THE
MYSTERY
AND
MAGIC
OF
LOVE

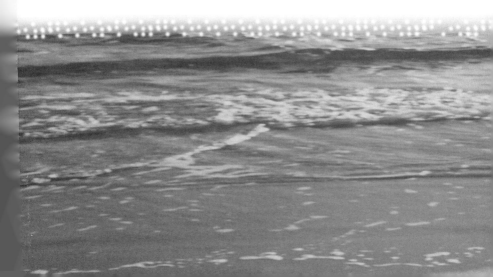

ALSO BY KRISHAN CHOPRA, M.D.

Your Life Is in Your Hands

🐚 🐚 🐚

OTHER HAY HOUSE TITLES OF RELATED INTEREST

<u>Books/Card Deck</u>

Beneath a Vedic Sky: *A Beginner's Guide to the Astrology of Ancient India,* by William R. Levacy

A Deep Breath of Life, by Alan Cohen

Heart Thoughts, by Louise L. Hay

The Love and Power Journal, by Lynn V. Andrews

The Love Book, by John Randolph Price

Secrets of Attraction: *The Universal Laws of Love, Sex, and Romance,* by Sandra Anne Taylor

Visionseeker: *Shared Wisdom from the Place of Refuge,* by Hank Wesselman, Ph.D.

Zen Cards, by Daniel Levin

<u>Audio Programs</u>

Relationships As a Bridge to Divine Love, by Barbara De Angelis, Ph.D., and Deepak Chopra, M.D.

There Is a Spiritual Solution to Every Problem, by Dr. Wayne W. Dyer

All of the above are available at your local bookstore, or may be ordered through Hay House, Inc.:

(800) 654-5126 or (760) 431-7695
(800) 650-5115 (fax) or (760) 431-6948 (fax)
www.hayhouse.com

THE
MYSTERY
AND
MAGIC
OF
LOVE

once the mind is infused with love,
only eternal joy is experienced

KRISHAN CHOPRA, M.D.
(1919–2001)

HAY
HOUSE

Hay House, Inc.
Carlsbad, California • Sydney, Australia

Published and distributed in the United States by:
Hay House, Inc., P.O. Box 5100, Carlsbad, CA 92018-5100
(800) 654-5126 • (800) 650-5115 (fax) • www.hayhouse.com

Editorial supervision: Jill Kramer • *Design:* Charles McStravick

Library of Congress Cataloging-in-Publication Data

Chopra, Krishan
    The mystery and magic of love / Krishan Chopra
        p. cm.
    Includes bibliographical references.
    ISBN 1-56170-857-7 (tradepaper)
    1. Love–Religious aspects. I. Title.

BL626.4 . C46 2001
291.5.677–dc21

                                                                    2001016923

ISBN 1-56170-857-7

04   03   02   01   4   3   2   1
1st printing, November 2001

Printed in Canada

To my wife, Pushpa, for her silent lessons in spirituality.
To our children—Deepak, Sanjiv, Rita, and Amita;
and our grandchildren—Priya, Mallika, Gauthma,
Kanika, and Bharat—for their unbounded love.

CONTENTS

PREFACE

Life is a mystery, solve it.
Life is a challenge, meet it.
Life is love, enjoy it.

— Mother Teresa

SOMEONE ASKED WHAT INSPIRED ME to write a book called *The Mystery and Magic of Love*. Quite simply, it was the unbounded and unconditional love showered on myself and my wife, Pushpa, by our children and grandchildren. When love is bestowed upon you, it fills your own heart with joy and brings you nearer to the source of love—whether you call it Higher Self, Spirit, Brahman, or God. Love is the source of unlimited potential, and it allows you to feel secure in the knowledge that you aren't separate from others.

🐚 🐚 🐚

Another name for love (or God) is *truth,* and the idea to write a book on the mystery and magic of love was further inspired by the story of Naciketas, which is based on one of the major Upanishads, entitled *Kathopanishad*.

The Upanishads, also known as *Vedanta* (sacred Hindu philosophical writings), contain legends and myths that illustrate the essence of moral and spiritual truth. They are precious gifts that remind us of our divine nature, and they have a timeless charm that continues to cast a spell on human life in our modern age. Ancient Indian sages believed that the Vedas—the Hindu texts of "real" knowledge—were created from the breath of God. These texts contain poetic invocations, prayers, and wise words that are relevant even today, explaining all that is needed for a peaceful and happy existence.

Naciketas was a young seeker of truth and happiness who sought to understand what love is. (My interpretation of the original story has been somewhat modified, without changing its fundamental premise.) He explores the realm of spirit, and asks the age-old questions: "Who am I?" "What am I doing here?" "Does heaven exist, and if so, how can I get there?" and "Is eternal peace, love, and happiness possible?"

I relate this story because I believe that if humankind is to survive, violence has to be replaced with love and compassion, which is the essential theme of Naciketas's story. But we must first endeavor to overcome fear.

Humankind has made tremendous advances in science and technology during the last century, particularly in the last 50 years or so. If this knowledge is properly used, it can help us abolish poverty, illiteracy, unemployment, and hunger. Unfortunately, these tremendous advantages have been (and are being) utilized to destroy humankind, too. The race for "power" that involves creating weapons of mass destruction is still on, and there's evidence of never-ceasing violence, its foundation based in fear.

Fear is created by an illusion that we're all separate. Out of fear is born insecurity, and this is the basis of greed, hatred, jealousy, anger, lack of contentment, arrogance, harsh words, untruthfulness, and "ego"—the root cause of negative emotion that is responsible for misery and unhappiness in the world.

The purpose of this book is *to spread the message of love*. Once the mind is infused with love, only eternal joy is experienced. Out of love—truth, honesty, and trust are born—which leads to charity, compassion, devotion, dedication, discipline, gratitude, contentment, the ability to forgive and forget, humility, speaking softly, and generosity.

The knowledge and wisdom of ancient and modern sages, saints, and thinkers, as shared within the pages of this book, will guide us to lead a life of love and fulfillment. Love should be the foundation of *all* of our thoughts and actions. Love of and for God manifests itself as love for our fellow beings, and *true* human love can reach great heights and become divine.

So let us all join on the journey to create heaven on Earth, where we play a game of love that ensures a score of love-all!

ACKNOWLEDGMENTS

My grateful thanks to Leon Nacson, publisher of *The Planet* newspaper in Australia, for his guidance, and for introducing me to Rachel Eldred, a brilliant and critical editor. I also owe my gratitude to Mr. Brij Mohan Tiwari for typing the script smilingly.

Special thanks to my colleagues: Dr. H. K. Chopra and Dr. K. K. Aggarwal; the staff of the Heart Care Foundation of India; and I. J. C. P. Group of Publications, New Delhi, for their love and spontaneous help, especially during the preparation of this manuscript.

Copyright permission to use excerpts is gratefully acknowledged. Thank you, Vikas Publishing House and Professor Mary T. David.

PART I

THE
RESTLESS SOUL
ON A
JOURNEY
TO
FIND
THE
TRUTH

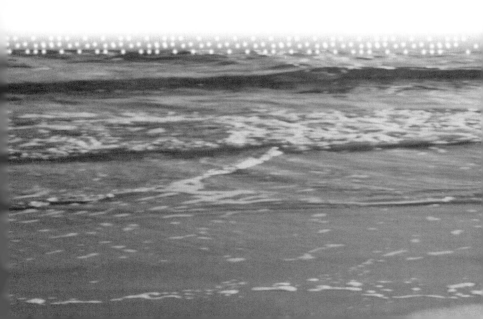

CHAPTER ONE

THE
JOURNEY
TO
HEAVEN

If you go to heaven without being naturally qualified for it, you will not enjoy yourself.

— George Bernard Shaw

VAJASRAVASA WAS KNOWN to be a learned man, and he had acquired knowledge of the scriptures from his father and other scholars. His father was famous for his wealth and wisdom and adored for his charity and compassion. During his life, he performed many rituals and sacrifices, and before he died, he gave almost all he had to charity. It was said that he had gone to heaven and attained immortality.

Vajasravasa knew about his father's prestige, and as he got on in years, he had a burning desire to be known and recognized as a great sage . . . although he knew in his heart of hearts that he wasn't. He was mortally afraid of death, but he knew he had to die one day (everybody has to), and when he died, he wanted to attain heaven. But in order to achieve this, Vajasravasa knew that he had to make a sacrifice, so he organized a

Yajna, a sacrificial ritual. He busied himself in preparing the Yajna, not realizing the significance and *real* meaning of charity and sacrifice.

Vajasravasa had created an image of himself as a learned man, although he knew his knowledge was very limited. He not only gave the impression, but announced openly, that he was going to renounce everything he had earned during his lifetime and give it away to the learned priests attending the ritual. However, he was not speaking the truth.

Vajasravasa's father had given everything away to charity without leaving anything to his son. But Vajasravasa had received a plentiful dowry when he married, and consequently had attained a lot of unearned wealth. Now, you may be able to cheat the whole world, but you can't cheat yourself. Vajasravasa knew he was posing to be something he wasn't—he wasn't giving away all he had; he was giving away what he no longer wanted, while quietly retaining whatever could be of use. (Even if people give away something they admire or like, but it's something that they have acquired by unfair means, it's not charity. The scriptures reject charity that's given by those who exploit others.)

Amazingly, Vajasravasa still thought he would attain heaven like his father. After the rituals were over and he gave away everything he possessed, Vajasravasa announced that he would go away to the forest to live the life of a hermit, meditating for his salvation. But in fact, he had no intention of doing so. He knew his son, Naciketas, loved him and wouldn't let him go to the forest and live by himself, and Naciketas knew that although his father's mind was on the ritual of sacrifice, he just didn't understand its implications.

Naciketas watched his father give away his cattle to the priests and other needy people, but he also knew that he was only giving away the old cows that yielded no milk. *What will my father attain by giving away these barren, old cows he doesn't even want anymore?* thought Naciketas. *This is no sacrifice. My father is doing all this for name and fame, and to attain heaven.*

Naciketas wasn't worried about his father's wish for fame and glory, or his wish to attain heaven. He was worried because he knew his father was aware of what he was doing and knew he would feel guilty later on. (There is no God waiting somewhere in heaven to punish you, but the feeling of guilt is a slow poison, and it can punish you directly and kill you in due course.)

"To whom will you give *me*, the last of your possessions?" Naciketas asked his father. Vajasravasa understood the true implications of this question, and in a fit of rage, exploded, "Unto death I give thee!"

And so it was that Naciketas left his father's house and reached the domain of death.

CHAPTER TWO

SACRIFICE IS
A
PILGRIMAGE
TO
GOD

Every act of sacrifice comes from love for God's creation.

— Jesus

W
HEN NACIKETAS ARRIVED at the portico of the palace of death, Lord Yama, the god of death and knowledge, was away on his rounds across the world. (In the Vedic period, Lord Yama wasn't considered a ferocious god or a threatening lord of bereavement. He was considered a philosopher and guide who escorts people to the gates of heaven.)

Naciketas waited three days and three nights for Lord Yama's return, and upon his return, Lord Yama listened to Naciketas's story. He appreciated his ideas on charity, sacrifice, and truth. He was also remorseful that a gifted, intelligent child who should have been treated as an honored guest wasn't looked after. Lord Yama thought it was a serious breach of hospitality—but Naciketas had declined food and drink when it was offered him because he wanted to meet with Lord Yama first.

Lord Yama declared that he would send Naciketas back to his father, and in return for his wisdom and patience, Lord Yama would grant him three wishes.

Naciketas, a dutiful son who loved his father dearly, said, "Lord Yama, I thank you for your decision to send me back to my father. For my first wish, I ask that my father be pacified, and that he recognize and accept me when I return." Lord Yama granted Naciketas his first wish, and assured him that his father would be happy to see his son released from the jaws of death.

For his second wish, Naciketas said, "In heaven, no fear exists. No one is afraid of old age. They have passed through hunger and thirst and moved beyond sorrow. You know what leads humans to heaven—please instruct me in it, for I want to know how the seekers of heaven attain immortality."

Here was Lord Yama's reply:

"Yes, I do know all about heaven and the knowledge that leads to it. I'm very pleased with your eager desire for knowledge about heaven.

"Heaven is not 'up there' somewhere in the sky, nor is it a faraway planet in another galaxy. Heaven and hell are states of mind—different planes of consciousness. You can live in heaven while mortal, and when you do, you won't be afraid of old age, and you'll see death as just one event in the continuum of life. Hunger and thirst won't bother you because you'll be in bliss, and your capacity to love and serve your fellow human beings will never diminish.

"To understand this, I will explain to you the knowledge of Agni (fire). Know that this knowledge is the support and strength of the universe, and is seated in the heart.

"The source of Agni is the sun. The sun emits heat and light, and is stored as energy. All life on Earth—plants, animals, and human beings—depend on it. It's the essence of life . . . but it can destroy life, too. The fire of attachment, when it turns toward reality (the truth) takes you to heaven on Earth. Here, in heaven, ego exists only in its subtlest form. The individual is forever flowing with divine qualities of love; and sees the beauty of love, selfless service, truth, gratitude, and the ability to forgive and forget. On the other hand, attachment to the material world will cause worry, anxiety, and transient pleasures.

"In ancient times, people worshiped the powers of the physical world—the sun, the moon, wind, rain, fire, heaven, and Earth—as well as the gods and goddesses who presided over nature. Some people in India still worship these gods and goddesses, but they understand that they're symbols, or expressions, of 'The One.' This form of worship was not only practiced in India, but also in Greece, Rome, and other ancient cultures where sacrifice and ritual were said to oppose the power of darkness, which robbed us of light (that is, the flow of truth and the way to heaven).

"'Outer' sacrifice and the rituals in the Vedas are used as symbols of 'inner' sacrifice and self-offering. We give what we are and what we have. We give what we have so the riches of divine truth and light may descend upon our lives and become the foundation of who we are, leading to right thinking, right understanding, and right action.

"Our sacrifice is a journey—a pilgrimage—toward God, truth, and reality, and we make that journey with Agni, the inner flame."

🐚 🐚 🐚

Lord Yama was impressed with the inquisitive mind and dedicated spirit of Naciketas. The boy hadn't expressed a selfish desire by asking for a wish for personal benefit, nor did he seek his personal liberation. He wanted to know how human beings could attain immortality. He was an ideal student, showing signs of spiritual blossoming. Lord Yama understood that what Naciketas *really* wanted to know about was the infinite, the eternal God principle.

Lord Yama decided to ordain upon Naciketas the "fire sacrifice"—which would henceforth be named "Naciketas Fire"—and he asked Naciketas to accept a garland of beads of different shades and hues as a gift. The garland would bless Naciketas with ego-nullifying powers, as well as unlimited energy for him to engage in the loving, selfless service of his fellow human beings upon his return to Earth. It would give Naciketas personal peace and tranquility under all circumstances, favorable or unfavorable.

Lord Yama explained the Naciketas Fire sacrifice to its namesake: He said it was the source of everything "good," and the destroyer of evil in the world. He further added, "Understand, Naciketas, I declare that whomever performs the sacrifice of Naciketas Fire three times, after understanding its significance, will attain everlasting peace and overcome birth and death." (There are many "threefold" factors in life—including mind, body, and spirit; father, son, and Holy Ghost; or Shiva, Brahman, and Vishnu—hence, the threefold Naciketas Fire for sacrifice.)

Lord Yama then realized that he had offered Naciketas three wishes, and asked him to request his third.

Naciketas said, "I have a doubt: When a man is dead, some say he exists and some say he doesn't. Which is it?"

"On this point, even the gods have had different opinions," said Lord Yama. "Naciketas, choose another wish. Do not press me on this."

"Lord Yama, I thought you had agreed to be my teacher. You have to grant me this wish—I have no desire for any other," replied Naciketas.

"Choose sons or grandsons who may live 100 years or more; request herds of cattle, elephants, horses, treasures of gold and jewels; or vast territory on earth. Ask for wealth and longevity. You can be King on Earth. I will satisfy your every desire, but don't ask me about the soul after death."

"All these things you talk about will decay. Even the longest life is short. I crave only for the wish I asked for," Naciketas implored.

Lord Yama was impressed, although not fully convinced that Naciketas was going to comprehend the intricate and deep knowledge concerning the soul after death, but Naciketas insisted that he was up to the challenge.

CHAPTER THREE

IN
PURSUIT
OF
KNOWLEDGE

They will come back again and again,
as long as the red earth rolls.
He never wasted a leaf or a tree,
do you think he would squander souls?

— Rudyard Kipling

NACIKETAS WAS CONVINCED that even if you live for one, two, or five hundred years, death lurks at the end, and you feel forever unsatisfied and incomplete unless you know what happens after death.

"Keep your chariots, your wealth, and your music, and teach me the knowledge that you agreed to share with me a little while ago," said Naciketas. "I know wealth can make a mortal comfortable, but he may not necessarily be happy. Happiness only comes when you know the purpose of your life and who you are."

Lord Yama was now convinced of Naciketas's sincerity to know all about self-realization. He knew that every human desire had been offered to Naciketas—including the dominion of the entire world—yet with the strength of his wisdom, Naciketas rejected it all because he was convinced that the transient could never reach the eternal.

Naciketas had all the qualities that a seeker of truth and love should have: He had a keen sense of discrimination (called *viveka* in Sanskrit); and, like a hansa, he could distinguish between real and unreal. (According to various legends, the snow-white hansa—a water bird found in the Himalayas—is endowed with a great sense of discrimination. It's said to be able to dip its beak into a mixture of milk and water and drink only the milk, leaving the water behind.)

Naciketas also had the spirit of "dispassion," which is the spirit of detachment to the fruits of his actions (known as *vairagya* in Sanskrit). He wouldn't run away from the world. He could be in the world but not of it. In other words, he didn't want to claim the world. His mind wasn't agitated, nor did he agitate the world. He was at peace with himself and at peace with the world. He had self-control. And above all, he had a deep, burning desire for self-realization. He knew that reality—the truth—has no substitute.

Lord Yama told Naciketas:

"Know the self as the lord of a chariot. Consider the human body the chariot itself, the intellect the driver, and the mind the reins. The senses are the horses and the sense objects are the roads.

"If the driver (the intellect) is indiscriminate and lets the reins (mind) loose, then the horses (sense organs) will run wild, hither and thither, along the road (sense objects). The chariot (body) shall be wrecked in sensuous excess and never reach the end of life's journey. But if the driver wants to enjoy this life and life hereafter, hastening his evolution, his sense of discrimination has to always be alert, with his mind always under control to guide the sense organs properly and reach the end of the journey.

"Above all else in life, human beings are motivated to be happy. This seems to be the ultimate goal. To get there, people follow one of two paths: One is the path of the good, the path of right, virtuous, and compassionate deeds; and the other is the path of the pleasant, the path that's pleasing to the senses or the mind. The path of the pleasant is more attractive. We want transient pleasures to come again and again, and if they don't, we experience pain and may adopt unfair means to obtain pleasure, which may not be in the interests of our fellow human beings. The path of the pleasant is the path of ignorance, while the path of the good is the path of knowledge.

"By following the path of the good, that is, not minding the unpleasant or the absence of immediate material gains, you rise up the rungs of the evolution ladder, and achieve lasting happiness and a state of enduring inner joy and peace.

"It's the ignorant who live in the midst of darkness. They choose to walk around deluded, and in many crooked ways fulfill selfish desires to accumulate wealth. They enjoy and suffer. They also forget their 'real' nature. The sense of ego, the 'I,' dominates and is the cause of suffering. The purpose of life and what happens after death doesn't bother such people. They are fooled by the glamour of wealth. Never happy, they fall again and again into the cycle of death and rebirth. As a matter of fact, a person like this usually feels hollow inside and, in spite of their hoarded wealth, is unhappy.

"Many people haven't heard of consciousness, the Higher Self, or the spirit, and many who have aren't able to comprehend it. A human being that can teach about the

Higher Self is wonderful, and equally wonderful is a pupil who can comprehend the Higher Self, consciousness, or Brahman (God). Learning about it or reciting its name isn't enough—one can only experience God when they understand life here and now, and life hereafter."

❦ ❦ ❦

Lord Yama was now fully convinced that he had found a deserving disciple who could understand and comprehend the eternal truth. It's well known that a teacher can sometimes become jealous of a brilliant student, so to counter against this, Lord Yama recited a peace invocation.

He then told Naciketas that the real seeker could discover truth and realize it as "this I am" (*avam ahum asmi*). It's an intimate personal experience, the reality that lies beyond the intellect, the ego of "I" and "me." The truth principle is the real "me." It controls and directs the body, mind, and intellect: It's the Lord of the chariot; it's the embodied soul. The embodied soul is like a wave in the ocean—it may be thought to be separate for a moment, but it isn't—it's the ocean. The embodied soul is the life spark that illuminates the body, mind, intellect, and ego.

Lord Yama said, "Just as the eye is an instrument to see other things with but can never see itself, the life spark—the soul—cannot be seen; it can only be perceived or experienced. Many ancient thinkers, scholars, poets, and philosophers think the soul is located in the heart, but that is used only as a metaphor. The soul is all-pervading, and it can be perceived and experienced through the regular practice of meditation.

"At one time, scientists didn't believe that the soul existed. Some even weighed the body before and after death to find no 'weight' difference. They concluded 'no soul' because nothing had left the body. A few of them admitted that the experiment illustrated that if there was a soul, it probably didn't weigh anything."

Lord Yama then went on to point out to Naciketas that the *Hiranyagarbha* state (Sanskrit for the "Golden Embryo"), as mentioned in the Indian scriptures, is the first stage of emergence into the manifest "material" world from the unmanifest. It's the sprout that peeps out at us to begin its journey as a tree. Similarly, other manifestations that constitute the universe are said to be supported by the state of Hiranyagarbha.

"It's been described as the 'wide opening of the dawn.' According to the ancient Indian creation hymns in the Vedas, it's the first born in the process of creation. It's the heavenly plane of consciousness in the realm of total or cosmic mind, and can lead to a process of gradual opening. According to the Vedas, there is a transformation well where the supreme reality, consciousness, or God ordains the unmanifest manifest. He is the Creator, and He is within us all. The material world, the galaxies, the stars, the forests, the rivers, and the whole world are expressions of the same supreme consciousness," said Lord Yama, concluding that "Hiranayagarbha existed prior to all other manifestations. It is the source of all that was, is, and will be."

CHAPTER FOUR

DISCOVERY

OF THE

ETERNAL TRUTH

Nothing in the world purifies like spiritual wisdom.

— Garland Sutra

LORD YAMA REMINDED NACIKETAS that eternal truth is subtler than the Hiranayagarbha state, but the seeker can realize it. The "this I am," realization is an intimate, personal experience that controls and directs the body, mind, and intellect. It is indeed ancient—it has never been born, nor will it know any decay or death.

The "atman" (or the truth) that vitalizes, controls, and directs the intellect, mind, and body, resides in the innermost recesses of the heart, which is the abode of Brahman.

After learning and grasping the idea of "reality," the subtle self in Naciketas rejoiced because he had obtained that which is the cause for all rejoicing. Lord Yama thought the abode of Brahman (God) was still open for Naciketas, and continued to fulfill his third wish.

Lord Yama went on to explain that everybody wants to go to heaven, but nobody wants to die because people are afraid of death.

"Before we discuss the question of what happens to you after you die, we must know who we are. Whose death are we talking of? Let's take a simple example that will explain the vital question of who we are, and subsequently what spirit, consciousness, and death are. Say, for example, that as a child you didn't like school, but then as you became an adolescent, you began to like it. You had more vigor and achieved goals and desires, but the "real" you didn't change—the "real" you observed the change. Say you're passing through old age now—whether you enjoy it or not is neither here nor there. The real question is, what are you observing?

"Your body and the physical world are subject to change, but the 'real' you, the observer, is the same, and is there throughout your life and death. The observer is your true self—immortal, silent, and nonchanging. This observer, the 'real' you, is what we call spirit, consciousness, or awareness.

"Beyond that, there is the state of divine consciousness—where you're 'in' the world but not 'of' it. This means you're reveling in the Higher Self while working in the world. Beyond that, you see your Higher Self (God) in every object—that is, God consciousness. And beyond that is unity consciousness, where the observer, the method of observation, and the object of observation are one— 'I am the universe (aham braham asmi).'

"To put it another way, beyond the senses is the mind, beyond the mind is the intellect, beyond the intellect is the embodied soul, and beyond the embodied soul is the spirit supreme, the super soul, the eternal reality. Once we realize that we're in eternal bliss and beyond all sorrow, we stop running after pleasure, and so we avoid falling into the snares of death.

"A seeker like you, Naciketas, can discover the eternal truth and realize it as 'this I am.' The real you, the soul, will never die, as it's not subject to decay or death. In the Bhagavad Gita, it states that just as a person discards old clothes to put on new ones, the embodied soul, having discarded the worn-out body, finds a new one.

"But problems arise when we identify ourselves with the body and the material world. The more you're involved in the material world—and the further away you are from the real you—the more you're tossed between good and evil, pleasure and pain, good and ill fortune. The pendulum swings between transient pleasures and the depths of despair.

"The knowledge of truth can also be called the true nature of self. All misconceptions disappear when the realization dawns that you are pure consciousness, or immortal awareness.

"We're not separate. You're in me and I'm in you, but our ordinary state of consciousness does not perceive this. Keep asking, 'Who am I?' Raman Maharishi says this is the only way to put an end to misery and usher in the truth.

"This doesn't mean that you have to renounce or withdraw from material life in order to cultivate the life of the spirit. The withdrawal advocated is that of a subtler kind. Peace of mind and bliss don't come through forcibly restraining the mind, but through allowing it to 'enjoy the inner,' thereby spontaneously withdrawing from the identification with, and excessive attachment to, the material world."

🐚 🐚 🐚

Lord Yama taught Naciketas that the truth is attained through meditation, and the awareness of self in meditation is called *samadhi* (being still). With this knowledge, Naciketas was able to reach enlightenment—a state in which samadhi is maintained along with *all* activity. The enlightened person sees self in everything and sees everything as the Higher Self. What does this person do now? There's a Zen saying that I feel is appropriate here: "He chopped wood and carried water before enlightenment; he chops wood and carries water after enlightenment."

Naciketas now knew that while one is engaged in worldly activities, they must abide in the Higher Self at all times. Naciketas, God's love, and God were the same. Naciketas was a self-realized man, a *Jiwan Mukta*. It was time to return home to his father.

When Naciketas returned, people of all ages gathered around, eager to listen to the story of his journey to Lord Yama. He told them everything that he'd learned from Lord Yama. Thereafter, the city became the city of joy. Love was the way of life. Everybody was affluent materially and spiritually, and neither sorrow nor suffering existed. Nobody was seen to be inferior to anyone else. The petty life of worry and jealousy was replaced by the everlasting life of sunshine, peace, and happiness. This, then, was heaven on Earth.

PART II

THE
MYSTERY
AND
MAGIC
OF THE
UNIVERSE, LIFE,
AND
LOVE

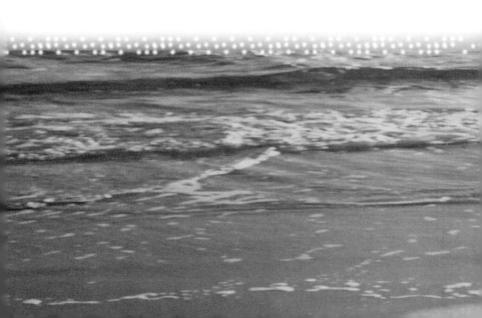

CHAPTER FIVE

ORIGIN
OF THE
UNIVERSE

*Who truly knows? Who can declare whence it was born,
whence was this manifestation?*

— Rig Veda

PARAMHANSA SRI RAMA KRISHNA (1836–1886), an
Indian mystic, once said, "The magician strikes his
wand and says, 'Come delusion, come confusion,
open the lid of the pot.' You see birds fly out and up, and
you enjoy it, although you know this so-called magic is a
trick. The magic is unreal, only the magician is real.

"Look at the galaxies, the forests, the hills, the
oceans, men young and old, me, you, and all beings
inanimate and animate. This is the real magic of the
divine love of the Creator."

🎔 🎔 🎔

In *Chandogya Upanishad*, it states that some people
believe that in the beginning, there was only Nonbeing, and
Nonbeing gave birth to Being—non-existence to existence.

Most people believe that Pure Being was here in the beginning—eternal and without beginning or end. Then Pure Being thought, *May I become many? May I take form and create light, the waters, and earth?* In this way, the entire universe was born from Pure Being.

All creatures are the manifestation of the same one "Being," but are aware of their individuality, whether they be tiger, lion, wolf, boar, human, or fly. All rivers, whether they flow to the west or east, have arisen from—and will return to—the ocean. They no longer think, *I am this river, I am that river.*

In the same way, all creatures, when they merge again into Being, don't remember that they arose from Being and went through life as this creature or that creature. It's just as if you were to take a pinch of salt and put it in a glass of water—the salt can't be seen, but it pervades every part of the water. Similarly, the Higher Self pervades every part of the universe.

Full of sap (its life energy), a great tree stands firm, drinking in and enjoying its nourishment. If the sap is withdrawn from a branch, the branch dies. If it's withdrawn from the whole tree, the whole tree dies. In the same way, when the spark of life (or the *prana*) is withdrawn from the body, the body dies, although the Higher Self lives on.

In the Bhagavad Gita, Krishna said, "If I remain at rest for one moment, this universe will be destroyed." (Krishna represents supersoul, consciousness, Brahman, or God—the unbounded potential of creative energy.)

Interestingly, the Sanskrit word for the "origin of the universe" translates as *projection,* not creation, which suggests a wavelike motion that continues throughout eternity.

Swami Vivekananda (1862–1902), the great Indian sage and reformist, said 100 years ago that although the word *creation* is used in the scriptures to refer to the origin of the universe, it isn't that the world was created at a particular time—that is, God didn't come, create the world, and then leave. No, the creative energy is still creating!

He went on to say that everything we see around us, or feel, touch, or taste, is simply a different manifestation of *akasha* (space). The earth, sun, moon, stars, forests, hills, rivers, our bodies, our minds, and our thoughts—the entire universe—has akasha at its foundation. A vital energy called *prana* acts on akasha, and the universe is projected into "reality." It has always been there in seed form, dormant in the ocean of akasha.

Swami Vivekananda explained the origin of the universe based upon ancient Indian scriptures. At the end of the 19th century—over three decades later—an American astronomer, Edwin Hubble, made a startling discovery based on scientific findings: The universe was expanding and galaxies were rushing away from each other at fantastically high speeds. He further found out that the larger the distance of separation between galaxies, the greater the speed. These observations suggested that once upon a time, matter in the universe must have bunched close together, squeezed into a solid ball of infinitely high density and temperature.

The Big Bang theory, currently the most accepted "origin of the universe" model in the scientific world, originated from Hubble's findings. Unlike other sciences, astronomy is observational rather than experimental, and all information gathered is derived from radiation measurements. *Radiation* is a general term that encompasses electromagnetic waves of all lengths: radio waves, millimeter waves, infrared light, visible light, ultraviolet rays, x-rays, and the extremely short gamma rays.

Until 1945, astronomy explored a very narrow window in the electromagnetic spectrum, but with the development of specialized space telescopes and sophisticated computer technology, scientists were able to gather more information about our universe. At the moment of the Big Bang, the universe is thought to have had zero size and infinite temperature. As the universe expanded, the temperature decreased rapidly to about ten thousand million degrees at the end of the first second. The universe expanded further, and 100 seconds later, after the Big Bang, the temperature fell a further one thousand million degrees.

Over the next million years or so, the universe continued to expand without any significant development. While the universe continued to expand, certain local regions, where matter was more dense, appeared as the result of a cease in gravitational attraction. (Wherever gravitational collapse occurs, an intensely dense object known as a "black hole" is seen.) Finally, the universe started to carry galaxies away from one another.

If the mass density of the universe is below a certain critical degree, then the universe will continue to expand forever. Alternatively, if it's above the critical value, the expansion of the universe will stop in a distant but finite time, and then the universe will start contracting and finally end up in a place known as *the big crunch,* and we'll start yet another cycle. According to some people, the Big Bang theory applies to only a *part* of the universe. There's a lot more that can't even be seen, even with great advances in telescopic equipment.

𝒔 𝒔 𝒔

What does the existence of the world, or even the universe, mean? It depends on what can be understood by *your* mind, and that of other human beings (that is, the Big Bang theory is an accepted model of the origin of the universe because it shares a collective understanding). It all depends on what we "perceive" of the world and the universe with our five senses.

Swami Vivekananda rightly points out that if we had another sense, we would perceive something else. Imagine for a moment that the human eye is equipped with a square lens instead of an oval one . . . the whole world would look completely different. A rabbit will perceive a marble according to the structure of its own eye, and it will be a completely different structure than what we see. A chameleon turns each of its eyes on a separate swivel, rather than together. We can't even remotely imagine the type of world a chameleon lives in.

As mentioned, the Big Bang theory is based on the findings of Edwin Hubble, who was able to see the stars at much greater distances apart because of his improved telescope. We can only imagine what else there is to be seen. Because of limited sense perception and the type of sense organs we have, we may not be seeing things the way they really are in the universe. We may also be seeing things that are no longer in existence. These are limitations of a fundamental nature, as is this question: What was there before the Big Bang? Yes, the struggle to find the origin of the universe is on, but its mystery and magic have yet to be solved.

Swami Vivekananda drew our attention to a somewhat similar origin theory as the Big Bang, expounded by the ancient sages of India a few thousand years ago. The concept is that the universe is *anadi ananta*—without beginning or end. The ancient sages said the entire universe is a process of breathing out and breathing in, which corresponds to alternating periods of manifestation and dissolution of the universe.

𝄞 𝄞 𝄞

If we were to pool together the wisdom of sages, seers, and philosophers of the past 2,000 years, and the knowledge of our modern thinkers, philosophers, and scientists, and submit it to critical analysis, we would reveal a universal truth. We would realize that the conclusions embody the crux of many noble sentiments, and in spite of apparent division, there exists *one* central unity among human beings. That is, we're not separate from each other and everything else in the universe, but are the manifestations of *the One*.

The Upanishads say that the origin of all is beyond past, present, and future, and is existent in the subtlest form within our minds. This is the One from which the entire universe evolves. The One who is everywhere, the universal witness.

In the *Shvetashvatara Upanishad,* it states: "Thou art the first, the sun, the wind, the moon, and the brilliant stars. Thou art woman, thou art man, thou art the maiden, thou art the old man tottering along with his stick. Thou art the deep blue butterfly. Thou art the green parrot with red eyes. Thou art the lightning. Thou art the seasons and the seas. Thou art the source of every source."

Once we understand this, then humankind's subtle and deep-rooted ego that sees itself as being superior, belonging to a superior race, can be overcome.

Unfortunately, to a large extent, our society reflects our individual dishonesty, manipulation, fear, greed, anger, hatred, frustration, and violence, activities that arise from an insecurity and discontentment with life, and with our belief that we're "separate."

On the other hand, if you have love for and of God, you hate no one, and love all creation. You're not separate from anyone, your mind is quiet, and your soul is peaceful. Your "ego" problem is subtle and can be dealt with. Once we realize that the purpose of life is to treat it with reverence, give to others, and love everyone, our individual and collective consciousness will ascend and be in touch with God or supreme consciousness. We'll know the *meaning* of life . . . even if we don't fully comprehend the *origin* of the universe.

♪ ♪ ♪

The Bhagavad Gita tells the story of Arjuna, who is given the divine eye so that the whole universe can be seen in Krishna. (Krishna represents the essence of everything, or God.)

Arjuna has a vision of Krishna—the cosmic, all-pervading, and universal divine—as not only the omniscient creator or omnipotent sustainer, but also as the all-powerful devourer of all names and forms, animate and inanimate. What Arjuna saw was in fact a sample of what is happening every moment. It can happen when the observer is beyond space and time, beyond the manifest and unmanifest.

Swami Chinmayananda, a sage and great teacher from India, said in the Bhagavad Gita that we should *realize* the truth and not be afraid of the *terrible* in the truth. In other words, we must recognize that the world is a combination of the beautiful and the ugly, the good and the bad, the soft and the hard, the sweet and the bitter, the animate and the inanimate.

God, the Lord, the One, has Himself become all of these, and therefore no adoration of the One will be complete if we recognize only the beautiful and the good. We have to recognize the Lord also in the ugly and the bad.

The fire leaps up toward the sky, toward its source. Rivers flow toward their source, the ocean. And humans, good, bad, and indifferent—including heroes, saints, and sinners—ultimately reach to their source. They all look for God, whether they know it or not.

CHAPTER SIX

ORIGIN
OF
LIFE

You must find quiet time to ponder the eternal mystery
of the birds in the sky, bees in the sun,
and flowers on a green hillside.

— Abraham Lincoln

THE STORY OF THE ORIGIN OF LIFE, as advanced by Charles Darwin in his theory of evolution, is rather speculative. To begin with, it's not even certain whether life originated on this planet or was transplanted here from elsewhere.

Nevertheless, according to Darwin's theory, Earth is supposed to be 4,500 million years old. It has a "reducing" atmosphere, and the ocean is like a healthy broth, with many minerals and salts dissolved in it. Chemical reactions, ultraviolet radiation, and thermal energy led to the formation of a number of complex molecules, including the self-duplicating DNA. Once these molecules, along with certain other compounds, were enclosed in a membrane, a cell-like structure resulted, and the unicellular anaerobic organism came into being. Gradually, with the release of oxygen from photosynthesis, and the availability of oxygen in the atmosphere, unicellular organisms came into being on land.

The origin of life was followed by slow evolution: Diverse and complex forms of living organisms developed from simple forms of life underwater and on land—from the unicellular organism to the multicellular organism. However, it's difficult to imagine that one major species could have evolved from another species. Authorities on the subject have stated that there is no evidence whatsoever to confirm that any major species arose from any other: Each one of them appeared as a distinct and unique creation. The skin and other faculties do change over a period of time—for instance, camels have developed a long neck and their pain threshold has changed so that they can graze on thorny leaves. But a dolphin has always remained a dolphin, and a human being is always human.

🐚 🐚 🐚

Albert Einstein revealed that each and every atom in the universe contains an enormous amount of power, and contemporary physics continues to demonstrate that everything in the universe comes into being through fluctuations in the underlying field of energy, which is the foundation of nature. This implies that there is *a single source of energy* that underlies everything, and it's from this source that all phenomena in the universe came into existence. As human beings, we're simply a localized concentration of energy in the universal field. The energy that flows through our bodies is the same as that which governs the universe. We're not separate. Everything is a part of nature, the continuum of the universe.

Atoms used to be considered the basic building blocks of everything in the universe, including our bodies. Quantum physics has shown that it's not so—atoms are *not* solid, irreducible objects. They're made up of subatomic particles: protons, neutrons, electrons, mesons, and quarks. These fine particles whirl around each other at lightning speed within each atom, and the distances between the subatomic particles are proportionately as great as the distances between various stars and galaxies. This implies that the human body and all other objects in the universe are as void as intergalactic space. The energy vibrations that make up our bodies—and everything else in the universe—are part of and within the universal field of energy, called *the unified field*. The universe is *vasudeva kutambam*, which means one family.

Yet scientists have not been able to convince themselves that the unified field is the ultimate source from which the universe and all life arises. They feel there may be a divine power behind the unified field. Einstein even remarked, "If only I knew the mind of God, the rest is only details."

🐚 🐚 🐚

Depending on whether our thoughts are positive or negative, they make different patterns in our brains and can be recorded with the help of positron emission topography. The thoughts are then converted into matter called neuropeptides. Sixty neuropeptides have been isolated from human blood. Thoughts of love and compassion are transformed into happy molecules, which give you a feeling of well-being and raise your immunity against disease, bringing you peace and happiness. On the other hand, negative thoughts—such as anger, greed, jealousy, and so on—make different patterns in the brain and are transformed into jittery molecules that circulate in your body and bring about misery and disease. Candace Pert isolated one of the "happy" neuropeptides while working at the National Institutes of Health (NIH): She called it Peptide T and said it raises the immunity of human beings so much that it can help to fight AIDS.

The idea that energy can be converted into matter (and that the equation can be reversed), was supported by the explosion of the atom bomb. Energy was used to create matter (the atom bomb) and in turn was transformed into huge amounts of energy (the explosion of the bomb).

Albert Einstein postulated that all fundamental forces of nature came from a field of dimensionless energy, which it transformed into matter: stars, forests, hills, rivers, human beings, the entire universe. He said that the universe has only one source, and he called this source the unified field. Einstein spent the last 30 years of his life trying to compute the mathematical formulation for the unified field.

Exploration of the subatomic world has revealed the intrinsic nature of matter. Subatomic particles don't exist as isolated entities but as integral parts of an inseparable network of interactions, involving a ceaseless flow of energy. These particles are whirling around at lightning speed, nearly the speed of light, during which they're created and destroyed. The protons, neutrons, and photons are stable particles, unless they're involved in collisions. When the transformation of neutrons to protons takes place, a new type of "massless" particle comes into existence. As I've already mentioned, the space between these particles is proportionately often as great as the expanses in intergalactic space, which signifies the fantastically minute size of these particles. It's also been noticed that these particles don't actually seem to be particles unless you're observing them closely. They otherwise resemble a wave or haze. Many more subatomic particles, like mesons, leptons, and quarks, are also involved in various sequences of collisions. Experimental photographs of such activity resemble the pattern of pictures depicting the cosmic dance, called *natraja*, of the Indian mythological god, Shiva.

Shiva has four arms superbly balanced, and yet the dynamic expressions demonstrate the rhythm and unity of life. The upper right hand holds a drum (*danru* in Sanskrit), symbolizing the primal sound of creation: With each beat of the drum, millions of galaxies are created. The upper left hand holds a flame, the element of destruction. The balance between creation and destruction is maintained. This is accentuated by the calm face, which signifies transcendence of the polarity of creation and destruction. The second right hand is raised in a manner symbolizing maintenance, protection, and peace, while the second left hand is pointing to the uplifted foot, symbolizing release from ignorance.

For modern physicists, Shiva's cosmic dance is the dance of subatomic matter. It appears that the entire universe is doing the dance of life. It's only that some "waves" are more alive than others. A stone, for example, is dancing the dance of life at the subatomic level, but isn't conscious of consciousness. It doesn't know it's a stone, and it can, one day, become a volcano or a diamond.

When the waves of "energy" become heightened, that is the beginning of intelligent life. Human beings are on top of the evolutionary ladder in that respect. We're "aware" of the awareness that we have, and that's why the restless human soul has been on a perennial search for the ultimate truth (that all is one).

The problem is that we perceive a limitation. This limitation is that we're *not* aware of what there is beyond space and time. But we can be in contact with "higher consciousness," which is beyond space and time. It's the real "I."

Author Deepak Chopra describes it like this: "As I go past the dark alleys and passages of my mind, I come to the core of my being. Here I am in touch with light and love, and the knowing that they are inherent properties of my natural state. At the core of 'being' and at the core of all 'beings,' there is a principle, an intelligence, that orchestrates and organizes the mind and body of all that lives. This principle, this pure intelligence, this pure awareness, this light of love, is unity consciousness. This intelligence at the deepest core of my being, other beings, and the universe has often been called God."

CHAPTER SEVEN

ORIGIN
OF
LOVE

O Divine Master, grant that I may
not so much seek to be consoled as to console.
To be understood as to understand. To be loved as to love.

— St. Francis of Assisi (1182–1226)

ANIMALS ARE THE ULTIMATE SOURCE of love and compassion. In their book *When Elephants Weep,* authors Moussaieff Masson Jeffrey and Susan McCarthy describe elephants crying, tears trickling down their wrinkled cheeks. This is a clear indication of the suffering experienced when they're captured and separated from their herds.

In another example, in Bangalore, India, Dr. Saghidahar Iyenger and his family nursed a wounded lion back to health; the lion grew so fond of them that when it returned to the zoo, it refused to eat unless encouraged by the family.

Dolphins, too, show compassion and unconditional love. They have been known to save humans from shipwrecks, and are recognized for their kindness and consideration. Likewise, gorillas have been seen to put their arms around each other and produce sounds as though they were singing. They stop eating if a mate is taken away or dies.

Animal attachment increases when animals are domesticated. Love flows to you from your pets, along with complete loyalty. This love is unconditional—pets don't ask questions or argue.

Animals also have no problem with "ego." If a horse or a dog wins a race, they might like it (because they receive praise from their owner), but they don't boast about it. A cow doesn't care if the color of her skin is black or white, or if her horns are beautiful or not, but her owner may. Ego is an issue only with human beings.

🐚 🐚 🐚

Humans, being the most evolved life form on Earth, have harnessed the resources of nature to suit them and their way of life, but the dictum expounded by Darwin of "survival of the fittest" has been carried too far. We have not only utilized the resources of nature to sustain us, but our demands are depleting nature's resources, even though we're quite aware that we rely on the continued bounty of Mother Nature.

Self-consciousness has been misappropriated to mean self-assurance and pride, and has been the source of ensuring and establishing one's identity and superiority over others. This mistaken notion—originating from the concept of "survival of the fittest"—has been responsible for every war throughout history, most notably World War II, where Adolf Hitler wanted to establish the superiority of a nation and race. And even today, wars go on in every corner of the globe due to this concept.

There seems to be a human urge to subjugate others, and an individual can become obsessed with dominion over others. But we have another choice: to live in love and harmony with others, and in turn, make life worth living.

To explain life's molecular basis doesn't come close to explaining the love and compassion that a spiritually evolved person has for his fellow beings. Such a reverence for life seems to come from the Higher Self, or pure consciousness, which is the spark of life, and no amount of chemical or molecular understanding can ever explain its origin. Toward the end of his life, Darwin himself realized that there was something more to life than chemical reactions and molecular chemistry, and he hinted that his explanation of the origin and meaning of life was inadequate. His interest in the beauty of life and music flourished, and he started to refer to a belief in the divine unseen power called God. In his autobiography, Charles Darwin wrote, "I was a young man with immature ideas. I threw out queries and suggestions, wondering all the time over everything. And to my astonishment, the ideas spread like wildfire. People made religion of them."

🐚 🐚 🐚

Everybody can agree that humans are the top rung of the evolution ladder; yet if you look around, it's quite clear that not all human beings have evolved in quite the same way. People exhibit great disparities in intelligence, love, morality, and other essential human aspects.

For example, some of us can't analyze a situation dispassionately, and are unable to discriminate between right and wrong. Still others seem to resemble vegetables: Like plants, they respond now and again, or may turn their head toward the sun, but they cannot think properly and are dominated by laziness (*tamas*). Other humans are like animals—they have not developed the faculty of discrimination, or a feeling of love for their fellow beings.

Among those who have evolved further, there are two types: the hawks and the doves. The hawks strive for possessions, pleasure, and power. They believe it does not matter if others suffer in the pursuit of their success. The doves, on the other hand, believe in the principle of "live and let live."

Finally, there are humans in whom divinity has become manifest. We can think of them as fully developed human beings. They can be called "divine humans" or "God humans." The Indian sage Swami Chinmayananda said, "They lighten the darkness of all that come across them. They enlighten them with the knowledge of life and living." He said it's possible for any human being to achieve this state if they live a *satwic* life (life of purity), have love, and hold the ideal of loving service. Only then can we unfold our inner glory, grow toward enlightenment, and say that God really did make human beings in His own image. Two of our role models here are Mother Teresa and Gandhi.

🐚 🐚 🐚

We can see that love is the greatest force of attraction, and it is the creative force behind fine arts, music, philosophy, and poetry, which are all attributes of God. In reality, our Higher Self is God, which is love. All God's creation floats in the ocean of love—not separate, but interconnected. All forms of life emerge from the one reality: God. How it all began, we don't really know. Let it remain a wonder, a wonder of all wonders.

CHAPTER EIGHT

THE
JOURNEY
OF
LIFE on the PATH
OF LOVE AND
RIGHTEOUSNESS

*There is no free lunch. Don't feel entitled
to anything you don't sweat and struggle for.*

— Marian Wright Edelman

IN MODERN SOCIETY, there are people who live for the moment and grab every opportunity for enjoyment. They have gathered many material possessions and live on the path of the pleasant.

For people who want everything, anything that's beautiful, satisfying, or enjoyable is seen as "good." Such people don't make any distinction between *the pleasant* and *the good*. In other words, they want to have a *good time* but aren't bothered about leading a *good life* (which in turn leads to lasting happiness). People who live the path of the pleasant sooner or later get fed up with their lifestyle and complain of feeling hollow inside, "wanting" something more. Their soul seems to know no peace.

The desire for worldly objects is the root cause of unhappiness; desire for pleasure can cause havoc. As author Jiddu Krishnamurti writes, "Pleasure is the guiding principle in our life. Pleasure is the thing we want most in this material world. . . . We want pleasure in any form and when the moments of excitement are over, the event is recorded in memory. Thought wants it to be repeated. But the trouble with pleasure is that it leads to and nourishes conflict that produces confusion. . . ."

Conflict ceases only when a person realizes that "I," the observer, and the observed object are one. Then the mind is silent, and a silent mind overrules the confusion.

In the Bhagavad Gita, Krishna said, "One who is like a little pond that swells when it rains and shrinks when there is no rain, is free from attachment, fear, and anger. The mind is like an ocean where rivers flow in and out, but the individual remains undisturbed. Such a person is called a sage of steady mind."

Since the beginning of time, happiness has been humans' main goal. The means to achieve this end have varied from time to time, in accordance with the views of ideologists, mystics, religious teachers, and philosophers, but the end result has been more often than not elusive. The search continues. . . .

Several decades ago, the unconventional and unorthodox way of life for a class of people from Bohemia in central Europe became popular all over the world. These people believed that to be independent from the conventional laws of society would make them happy; subsequently, a large number of people all over the world sought happiness the "bohemian" way. They developed their own fads and were interested in psychedelic experiences. A disorganized lot, they had no proper work to do, and a large percentage of them formed a dependency on drugs. But the search for happiness that way proved futile, and the movement gradually died a natural death—there must be other ways to find happiness.

🐚 🐚 🐚

A patient of mine named Jagan Nath was more than 60 years old when he first came to my office for consultation for his asthmatic complaints about 25 years ago. He'd given up smoking ten years previously, but the residual effects bothered him off and on. He worked in real estate, and was a well-known and successful builder. The high-rise buildings he built were in great demand. A hardworking, conscientious man, he made a lot of money the *right* way. Jagan Nath died at around 85, leaving a huge fortune to his only son, Jiwan.

About six years after his father's death, Jiwan's wife, Usha, made an appointment for her husband to see me. I was surprised when I saw him, for he had grown old since I'd seen him last. He was obese, with a potbelly and very high blood pressure. Not surprisingly, the electro-cardiogram (ECG) scan came back showing signs of coronary heart disease.

Usha told me that Jiwan had inherited a great deal of real estate and money, and soon after his father's death, he closed his real estate office, which wasn't doing as well as it had been a few years earlier. "Why should we bother?" Jiwan insisted. "There are millions in the bank, and if we need more, we can sell a property."

He traveled to Switzerland, roamed Europe, went to America, and stayed in five-star hotels. Jiwan started drinking a lot—starting his days with Scotch or whiskey—and going to gambling dens. He began throwing lavish cocktail and dinner parties for his friends. Jiwan thought all this would make him happy, but his insatiable desire for pleasure didn't bring him any happiness. He never exercised, and consequently developed diabetes, high blood pressure, and insomnia.

Usha then went on to tell me that their only grown daughter had been influenced by his habits and kept him company during his drinking sessions. Understandably, she was worried. "I only wish we didn't have all this wealth," she said. "We are very unfortunate to have inherited this fortune."

This is but one story about the bane of wealth: It cannot and does not guarantee happiness.

♪ ♪ ♪

According to various people, happiness comes from volition, exercise, and the power of free will. Real contentment and happiness will only come when you have *complete* freedom. That includes liberation from addiction or attachment to material possessions.

All religions guide you toward peace and happiness. For instance, Christ gives a declaration on blessedness, promising happiness and peace to the poor in sprit, the mournful, the seekers of righteousness, the merciful, the peacemakers, the pure of heart, and the sufferers of righteousness when they surrender to the Lord. In other words, the Christian idea of blessedness (contentment and happiness) is one way to God, who is love. What follows is bliss, which is deeper and purer than happiness because it's free from the accidents of time and the circumstances that happiness is exposed to.

Indian sages term the highest form of joy *ananda*. Ananda must be differentiated from *sukh*, or happiness. It's beyond happiness, and those who meditate upon God ultimately experience ananda or bliss, which is limitless, immutable, and permanent, while happiness is limited, mutable, and impermanent. Happiness is a state that oscillates between the dualities of pleasure and pain, while ananda transcends the nature of duality.

♪ ♪ ♪

The philosopher Søren Kierkegaard (1813–1855) believed that there are three stages of life. The first stage he called the *aesthetic stage* (the story of Jiwan relates to this stage). In due course, people in this stage become slaves to their desires—they're often vain and egotistic, boasting selfish desires. These people suffer from feelings of emptiness and fear, which further aggravates "negative" emotions, including guilt. This can lead to change: The individual can decide to shift from the aesthetic stage to the *ethical stage,* or directly to the *religious stage*. Many choose the ethical stage and subsequently follow the path of the good rather than the path of the pleasant.

Any person can change from the aesthetic stage to the ethical stage if they learn to have self-control and discipline. But is this too difficult? No, not if we recognize that each individual soul comes with an ego and must contend with the material world in a physical form. Every human has the divine *and* the devil within him, and the battle between them goes on all the time. The best way to make peace is to attempt to move toward union with the Higher Self. The energy for this comes from the exercise of self-discipline, which means we must control our physical appetites and passions.

Most people consider the term *self-discipline* to be something grim. They think it's the domain of a monk or a soldier—yet all members of a football team are disciplined. They exercise regularly and have disciplined eating habits, and everybody appreciates that. But *we* have to be self-disciplined and moderate in our own eating, sleeping, and working habits if we're to have healthy bodies, minds, and intellects; happy lives; and peace. We must resist quick gains; we must be taught not to talk big and act small; we must set a goal in life and then get busy in the dreary details that are essential in order to achieve it.

Every stressful situation should be treated as an opportunity. As you move up the ladder of success, don't think *more stress,* think *more opportunities.* You may not be able to change the direction of the wind, but you can certainly adjust the sails. Self-discipline gives you joy and a sense of achievement, and allows you to drop self-destructive habits automatically.

By the same token, you will do well in life and achieve peace if you give credit to others for your success. Don't work for money or power alone. It won't save your soul, it will only boost your ego, which brings misery in the long run. Don't be afraid of failing: It really doesn't matter how many times you fall, what matters is how many times you get up.

If you run in the fast lane all the time, you're bound to stumble at times; therefore, move slowly in life. Let the river of life flow. On one bank of the river is pleasure; on the other side is pain. You're bound to bump from side to side, and that's okay. Don't get stuck on the bank of pleasure—it's never permanent. You're bound to lose it, and as a consequence, experience pain.

🐚 🐚 🐚

Before Jesus commenced his mission of teaching, preaching, and healing, the Holy Spirit led him to the desert, where the Bible says that Jesus spent 40 days and 40 nights fasting. The devil (temptation, ego) came to him and said, "Why are you starving? You know you can perform miracles. Look at those smooth, round stones lying all over the desert—you're the son of God, and you know you can convert those stones into bread. Go ahead, do it, and satisfy your hunger." Jesus knew he could do it, but he told the devil, "Yes, but a person does not live on bread alone, but on every word that comes from the mouth of God."

After his period of fasting was over, Jesus received five loaves of bread and two fish from a young lad. He blessed the food and asked the disciples to distribute it to the people who had collected there . . . there were 5,000 of them. Jesus showed love and compassion to the poor and the needy; he performed miracles for them, but never to satisfy his personal needs or ego.

The ego temptations that came to Jesus in the desert come to us every day. We all want to conquer the material world and rule it, too. Let us all pray to God that with His grace we can face the temptations of our ego and overcome them so we're able to sacrifice our comfort to serve the needy with love.

In the Bhagavad Gita, it states that a disciplined human is one of moderation. He neither sleeps too much, nor is he awake the entire night. He never overeats, nor does he starve often. He has reverence for the Holy Spirit, his parents, teachers, and the sages. Straightforwardness, harmlessness, physical cleanliness, and sexual purity are his virtues. He speaks without ever causing pain to another, and he is truthful, always saying what is kind and beneficial.

🐚 🐚 🐚

According to ancient Indian traditions, there are four *pursharthas* (goals) in life: dharma, kama, artha, and moksha. Dharma is not synonymous with religion, but is the essence of all religions—it's the path of righteousness. Some people follow it scrupulously, knowingly or unknowingly, all their lives.

The word *dharma* is derived from the Sanskrit word *dhri*, which means "to uphold or sustain the existence of a thing." It can be said to be the law of being, the essential property or characteristic of something.

Dharma has two levels: an individual level and a cosmic or universal level. At the individual level, one is an artist, musician, physician, or farmer. The duties one has to perform are one's *swadharama* (*swa* literally means "individual").

At the universal level, however, dharma is common to *all* human beings. It's what distinguishes humans from all other beings, and is called *manava* dharma (*manava* actually means "human"). We recognize the divinity that's already deep within our being. Everything in creation is essentially divine, but it's given only to human beings to fully manifest the divinity within us and become divine. Once we do so, we enjoy unbounded freedom and bliss.

Dharma, or the path of righteousness, forms the basis of our individual progress and social welfare. It's the first of all four goals in life, and we have to be on this path the entire time while we achieve the other goals: artha (acquisition of wealth), kama (satisfaction of desires), and moksha (spiritual fulfillment). All these goals constitute an integrated scheme, which involves the attainment of both mundane success and spiritual well-being.

Artha, acquisition of wealth, is an important goal for a successful life, provided its acquisition and utilization is in accordance with the principles of dharma. Wealth, material and spiritual, has to be shared—it's required to look after your body, family, and community; to assist educational institutions, hospitals, and other public works; and to promote art and music. It must circulate, for if hoarded, it stagnates and promotes greed.

The third goal is *kama,* or desire. It doesn't apply only to sensual enjoyment—all legitimate desires are selfless and benefit the people around you, giving you satisfaction and inner peace.

Sensual enjoyment has been assigned an important place in life, provided it's in accordance with the dictates of dharma. Life would become dull and boring without the senses, and pleasure pursued in accordance with dharma creates a genuine yearning for spiritual fulfillment and freedom.

The outright materialist only believes in two goals: artha and kama. He spends his life pursuing these goals. In India, there was a school known as the "Charvaka" school, which advocated outright materialism, rejecting righteousness and spirituality. But whoever follows this path is often left feeling dissatisfied, incomplete, empty, and hollow. On the other hand, the person who aspires to lead a good and worthy life, without merely desiring a good time, will examine his behavior until laziness and unruly passions have been subdued, and the *satwa* (purity and discipline) radiates through.

The Bhagavad Gita teaches that real happiness is happiness of the spirit. At the beginning of a self-disciplined life, things may appear dull and devoid of attraction, but in the end, *moksha* (peace and bliss) prevails. Moksha is liberation due to spiritual fulfillment. The word is derived from the Sanskrit verbal root *mus*, which literally means "to release or set free." This state eradicates all passions (*kelasha*) and cravings (*trishna*), and can also mean "blown out" or "extinguished."

One who is above good or evil is said to have attained moksha, or *bodhi*, *nirvana*, or *kaivalya*. It's the realization of the Self by the Self. It is the state where death and birth, and the recurrence of desire, pain, and pleasure don't matter, for you're in a state of supreme peace.

CHAPTER NINE

HUMAN LIFE:
A
PILGRIMAGE
FROM THE
WOMB to MOKSHA

Your children come through you, not from you.
You may give them your love but not your thoughts.

— Khalil Gibran

IN INDIA IN ANCIENT TIMES, love in marital relationships was considered sacred. The warmth of parental
love was known to have tremendous beneficial
effects on the children. It was believed that true love
between parents better prepared the soul for incarnation,
and resulted in a more enriched development of children
after conception. The ancient sages believed that the
effects of love on children started even before conception, just as they believed that angry and ill-tempered
persons shouldn't visit the fields before the crops were
sown. Instead, innocent children should be taken there
to play, because plants are alive and respond to human
voice and emotions, innocence (love) is a powerful
energy, and purity is a valuable fertilizer for plants and
human beings.

There are various Indian legends that illustrate that the feelings, emotions, and learning processes of the baby actually start in the womb. I would like to relate one such story here about Asthavakra, which has been adapted from the great mythological epic *Mahabharta.*

Asthavakra's father, Kohor, was a great scholar and lived in the kingdom of Rajrishi Janak, who himself was well versed in the Vedas, Upanishads, and other sacred texts. While Asthavakra was still in the womb of his mother, Kohor would sit by her side and recite the Vedas.

One evening, the child in the womb said in a loud voice, "Through your grace, Father, I have learned all the Vedas while in my mother's womb, but I'm sorry to say that you often make mistakes in the recitation and interpretation."

Kohor was shocked. He didn't understand what his son had said, and in a fit of rage, cursed him. He screamed, "You will be deformed in eight places when you're born!"

When the child was born, he was indeed deformed and twisted in eight places; hence, he was named *Asthavakra,* which means "to be bent in eight places like a camel." After his birth, Asthavakra kept studying, and by the time he was 12 years old, he was a great scholar.

One day, Kohor was invited to King Janaka's court for a debate. The participants were to interpret and discuss passages of the Vedas.

Asthavakra heard that his father was losing to a scholar named Vandin in the final round. He went to the court of King Janaka but wasn't allowed to enter the hall of the great debate. He eventually managed to get in, and as he was walking through the hall, the pundits (the so-called scholars), upon seeing the boy with the crooked body and funny walk, started to laugh. Asthavakra started to laugh even louder. Upon hearing him laugh like that, there was silence. Everybody started to wonder what was there for the boy to laugh at. King Janaka finally said to the boy, "I understand why these people laughed, but I don't see why *you* laughed. My child, I want to know why you laughed."

Asthavakra replied, "I was amazed to find that you have invited so many uneducated people here, Your Majesty. You call them scholars, but they see only my body and not the one who lives in that body. In any case, they can't really be scholars if they laugh at somebody's physical disability."

King Janaka came down from his throne, apologized to Asthavakra, and asked him to sit in the court hall. The king then requested that Astavakra clarify some of his own questions. First, he wanted to know about a dream he'd had the previous night. In the dream, he was a beggar, weeping and wailing, for he couldn't afford to look after or feed his wife and seven children. The king offered a detailed account of his life as a beggar—it seemed like a lifetime had passed when he suddenly awoke and realized he had slept only for a short time.

"What I want to know is," the king asked, "am I a king who dreamed that I was a beggar, or am I a beggar having a dream now that I am a king?"

Asthavakra replied, "We're aware of three states of consciousness: the waking state, the sleeping state, and the dreaming state. None of these are real. You, the *real* you, experiences constant change. Childhood, youth, middle age, old age, even death—these are all changes in the continuum of life. Even the states you pass through every day—the waking state, the dream state, and the sleep state—are different from the body that experiences these states. A person who lives in a house is not the house.

"There is a 'being' in you who knows about the waking, dream, and sleep states, and he witnesses everything that happens in these states. Who is the being who remains awake in all these states, that is, who reports your dream to you when you wake up, and lets you know that you slept well? Who is that 'knower' who is fully conscious in all states? This is the 'eternal principle.' To be aware of this awareness, to become aware of this witness (*sakshi*) in you, and to identify with it, is the only way to know who you are."

♪ ♪ ♪

The legends of yesteryear, such as the one related above, illustrate that the feelings, emotions, and learning processes of the baby start in the womb and continue throughout childhood. As parents, it's our love that will guide our children, but our contradictions do so, too. For instance, we tell lies, but tell our children not to lie. We smoke, but tell our children not to smoke. We indulge in alcohol abuse and tell our children, "This is an adult drink"—so children can hardly wait for adulthood. Should we not set examples that our children can follow with love, compassion, and kindness?

Modern parents usually have tight, stressful routines that lower their immunity. Hence, for your children's future, you have to learn to manage your stress. We must remember that our children are always watching us. They will find out our shortcomings as they grow up, but as Oscar Wilde put it, "Some of them will forgive us." The point is, if we show our children the very best we can be, we can make this world a better place for future generations to live in.

Nurturing a child in the womb plays a vital role in determining the child's future lifestyle and intelligence. This has been demonstrated by scientific research, which also suggests that genetic determinants are frequently over-valued in relation to a child's future IQ levels. Recent studies have quashed the idea that genes determine a child's intelligence more so than environmental factors, indicating that nature does not overwhelm nurture in relation to infants.

It may sound strange, but neuroscientists and researchers are discovering that educating the baby in the womb, and for a two-year period after birth, is the most crucial time in shaping the child's future life. On the other hand, fighting between parents has been shown to retard the growth of the baby's brain while in the mother's uterus.

It's been shown that billions of neurons grow in the brain during the early life of the baby in the womb. The first spurt in brain cell growth occurs during weeks eight and thirteen of life. The record spurt starts ten weeks before birth. There are more than 100 billion neurons present at birth, and the growth of these neurons continues for two years afterward. While the number of neurons is important, it's the synapses—the connectors between these cells—that are responsible for creating a strong foundation for emotions, feelings, sight, hearing, and most psychomotor skills.

The behavior of people in the home, an atmosphere of love between the parents before and after conception, education of the child in the womb, and the love given in early childhood greatly influence the child's physical and mental growth.

Love at this stage of life can be magical. The conditioning of the comparatively clean "I" consciousness begins, and the child is increasingly influenced by its environment. The mother tells her child that she is very beautiful and has the most exquisite eyes in the world—consequently, the child is convinced that she *is* beautiful, and the ego starts to take over.

As a child's personality develops, the sense of ego—"I am"—unfolds further. Children learn to respond to their names, recognize their faces in the mirror, and start determining what "beautiful" really means. As they learn to walk, they become conscious of their power—the ego is becoming ever more important. Guidance and education by teachers in early childhood molds the child even further.

Then a child is influenced by their school environment, peers, TV, computers . . . there are countless conditioning factors. As the child grows up, he or she is identified as a boy or a girl, then as a man or a woman. The child is identified as intelligent or stupid, beautiful or ugly, highly intelligent or illiterate, belonging to a wealthy or a poor family. The child, who is now an adult, may be full of compassion and love; or be selfish, greedy, and jealous. The child is the end result of conditioning at all stages in life, starting before conception. But who *is* the child really?

A number of spiritual teachers refer to developing detachment from worldly objects, and teach that you should treat pleasure and pain the same way and not bother about either—but that's easier said than done. To remain uninfluenced and unfettered by worldly pulls, to be detached, and to show least concern when a human experiences pleasure or pain requires an extraordinary capacity for understanding and detachment. Invariably, we become elated when something good happens and get depressed when sorrow affects us. It requires deep knowledge of our Higher Self and the transient nature of our senses. Once you realize that, then you might develop what could be termed "detached attachment," dispassion, or *vairagya*, in Sanskrit.

🐚 🐚 🐚

There is no need to withdraw from the material world to lead a spiritual life—after all, the material world includes your body, mind, and intellect. Withdrawing from the material should be subtle and include renunciation of your lower self, which includes jealousy, hatred, the inability to forgive and forget, and above all, ego, which is the fundamental cause of unhappiness and misery. In the *Isha Upanishad,* it's emphasized that real fulfillment comes from living a full material existence *and* a full spiritual one. To illustrate, I'd like to relate the story of Saint Augustine.

Saint Augustine was a great saint. He had spent his entire life in search of inner peace. Early on in his life, he looked for satisfaction in worldly pleasures, and pursued different spiritual practices. He wandered from one city to another and from one forest to another. He studied every book on religion and science, but the burden of this acquired knowledge became heavy, so he was not at peace.

There were days when Augustine's mind was quite turbulent. Once, he was walking by the ocean when he saw a young, rather anxious boy standing on the sandy shore holding a cup in his hand. Saint Augustine approached him and said, "You look very depressed. Can I help you?"

The boy replied, "I'm trying to find out how I can fit the ocean in my cup. The ocean is so big that no matter what I do, I can't contain it in my cup and take it home!"

"Then why don't you throw your cup into the ocean?" asked Augustine. As he said this, he had a flash of insight:

He realized he had been trying to contain the infinite bliss of God in the tiny cup of his ego. The moment he realized this, he threw away the cup of his ego, and from that very moment, he knew that he could hold the ocean— the infinite bliss of God—in his individual embodied soul. His individual soul was no longer a wave; it was indeed the ocean.

Every one of us is like that little boy. Millions of us are standing on the shore of that vast ocean of consciousness holding out the cups of our egos. We keep looking at each other, feeling jealous because the other person's cup is bigger, filled with more "material" possessions. We don't give a thought to the idea that however big the cup of our ego may be, it simply can't contain the vast ocean of consciousness.

Once you abide in the Higher Self and leave ego behind, you are in bliss. You have achieved *moksha*, which is liberation.

PART III

THE

BATTLE

OF

LIFE IS ONE

OF

CONTRARY DESIRES

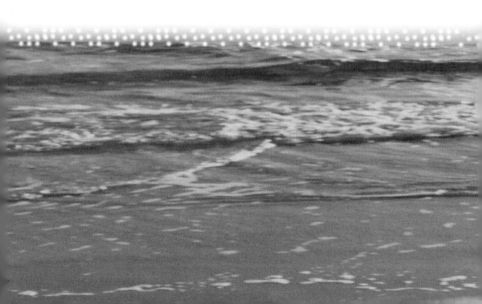

CHAPTER TEN

JEALOUSY
AND
NONFULFILLMENT
OF
DESIRE LEADS
TO
ANGER

No man thinks clearly when his fists are clenched.

— George Jean Nathan

IN THE STORY OF NACIKETAS (FROM PART I), we learned that his father, in a fit of rage, gave Naciketas to the lord of death. Most of us can somewhat relate to this story, because in anger, we often do things that in hindsight we really wish we hadn't.

Take the case of Sham Nath and Chander, for instance. Both men are well-to-do businessmen, and they're also neighbors. Sham Nath didn't like Chander parking his new Mercedes next to Sham Nath's house instead of his own. Chander insisted that there was more space next to Sham Nath's house, that his car didn't bother anybody, and that it was on corporation land anyway. Sham Nath liked his neighbor's Mercedes very much, but didn't appreciate the show of wealth—jealousy was the root cause of his frustration.

Jealousy, like nonfulfillment of desire, leads to anger. It's a common human emotion, and like other "negative" feelings, its basis lies in insecurity. You feel left out and imagine your colleagues or neighbors doing better than you.

Keep in mind the old saying that the grass is always greener on the other side of the fence: It may not really be so, but you think it is. For instance, you go to a restaurant with your friends or family, order the dishes you like, and after they're brought to the table, you look at the dishes being served at the next table and wish you had ordered those.

Your neighbor's wife looks more attractive than your own wife does, although you may not know that they're about to get a divorce. You become jealous of your colleague because he's doing better financially than you, even though you think you're more clever than he is. Husbands have been known to become jealous of their own wives when they perceive that their spouses are achieving more than they are in art, literature, or business. A brother will become jealous of another sibling who seems to be their mother's favorite, and so on.

"There are two tragedies in the world," said Oscar Wilde. "The first is to want to have what you don't have, and the second is to have it."

In *Kathopanishad,* Lord Yama was fully convinced that Naciketas, after a few sessions of teaching, was a deserving disciple who could understand and comprehend eternal truth. He also recognized that a teacher may become jealous of such a brilliant student, so he recited a peace invocation.

Lord Yama was a master teacher, and Naciketas considered himself lucky to have found a teacher like him. For his third wish, he rejected all offers of material wealth and comforts and insisted that Lord Yama give him the knowledge of the mystery of life and truth, beyond what we can perceive with our senses. The master teacher, profoundly humble, saw nine-year-old Naciketas as his equal and knew he was ready for the knowledge. From this story, we learn that you attract what you're ready for—in some cases, that can be divinity; in others, it may be anger and jealousy.

Returning to Sham Nath and Chander, the fighting neighbors continued to argue about the parked Mercedes. One afternoon, a particularly serious confrontation erupted into fisticuffs. Afterward, they independently lodged complaints with the police. I came to know about this case when they were brought to the emergency room in the hospital where I work. More than a year after the incident occurred, the case is still in court. Both men refuse to reach an out-of-court settlement because each one thinks he is right and the other is wrong.

Someone suggested to Sham Nath that he would have been better off if he'd turned his back on Chander, and instead of hitting him, walked into his house and beat his pillow. *What? Beat a pillow!* Sham Nath never could have done that! How could he even think of expressing his anger via his pillow? Everybody around him would have thought he was a coward. His ego would never have allowed him to run away from the scene of battle. Plus, Sham Nath actually wanted to kill Chander, but he held back, as he was conscious of the fact that if he did, he'd end up in jail for the rest of his life. So much for "love thy neighbor."

We all know that trifling incidents like the above have often ended in one or more people being seriously hurt or even killed. In a fit of rage, the mind is confused, and a sense of discrimination simply doesn't exist. Anger is a slow poison that has a cumulative effect on your body—eventually you explode, and whoever is in close range of your fury may become the victim of your anger, even after a seemingly insignificant quarrel. Arguments occur because the belief system of the person arguing is so strong that the mind is closed to anything else. But keep in mind that you *always* have the choice to discuss things with an open mind.

🐚 🐚 🐚

The true nature of a human being is to be happy, because the source (consciousness, eternal reality) is bliss. Like the ocean, there are millions of waves, some big, others small, and they're influenced by the external world. Winds, sun, climate, and other external factors affect it, but deep down, the ocean is calm. Underneath the surface, there are no storms, waves, or even ripples. The mind can be likened to an ocean: You're bound to experience events that can generate anxiety, jealousy, or anger. If you remain at the "surface" of the ocean, you can't change or control these provoking winds, but you can, of course, fight them.

When the ocean fights the strong winds, bigger waves arise. Similarly, if you fight, your anger and confusion worsen, and your sense of discrimination disappears. On the other hand, if you suppress anger, all it will do is change direction. Such emotion is difficult to control if you tell yourself, "Don't be greedy, don't hate anyone, don't be angry"—for instead of releasing your anger, you'll end up retaining it. You'll nurture it until it finally bursts.

Rather than repress anger, it's best to defuse it, or, better still, transform it with love. Every time you're angry, a number of chemicals (such as catecholamine, adrenaline, and non-adrenaline) are released into your body, raising your pulse rate and blood pressure, making your muscles tense, and automatically triggering rapid breathing through the mouth. If you're often angry, in due course you'll accumulate an overabundance of these chemicals, and will probably come across as a grumpy, irritable person. Violence will erupt in your speech and even eating habits. Aggressive behavior will be noticed in most actions you perform—you'll tend to slam doors and do things abruptly—due to an overaccumulation of chemicals in your blood.

These same chemicals cloud the intellect. The mind becomes confused and loses any sense of discrimination. It's a commonly observed occurrence that someone caught in the grip of anger doesn't heed good counsel. Only a reposed mind and a clear intellect can discriminate between good and bad or right and wrong, and also understand and foresee the consequences of particular decisions and actions. Repeated violent or angry episodes move you down the rungs on the ladder of evolution. Instead of *e*volving toward enlightenment, you *de*volve.

The question still remains: How do you prevent anger and defuse it? Some people feel that there is nothing wrong with going into the backyard and screaming, as long as it's not directed at anyone. Surprisingly, there is no evidence to prove that getting things off your chest has any beneficial effect. And as we've seen, suppressing the anger doesn't help, either. So, what can you do?

The best way to counteract anger is to hold your breath momentarily; and then take slow, deep breaths through the nose—this stops the panic reaction, calms you down, and puts you back in the control seat. Suddenly, you won't feel so completely out of control. Deep and slow breathing allows the life force (or *prana*) to have a direct and calming effect on the emotions, and it may short-circuit an oncoming fit of anger.

If someone is annoyed with you, their anger can be defused if you make them laugh. Arguments are usually unnecessary and are effectively dissolved with humor. If you can see humor in difficult and/or serious situations, it allows you to think properly, make the right decisions, and help extinguish anger. If you smile most of the time, you just can't be an angry person.

🐚 🐚 🐚

Music also helps to defuse anger. The whole universe is alive with music, and the sounds are but its frequencies and vibrations. Today, composed music can include animal sounds—including the songs of whales or the chirping of birds, the murmuring of rivers and streams, the ebb and flow of the ocean, and the rustling of the wind through the leaves. The *soothing* effects of these sounds remind us that everything in nature is interconnected through sound and music. For this reason, if we take time every day to chant or listen to quiet music, we'll promote a quietude of mind that will quell any upcoming waves of anger.

The harmful chemicals released into the bloodstream during an episode of anger—or accumulated during moments of feeling angry—can be used and harnessed to generate zeal, determination, and perseverance, instead of leading to irritability, agitation, and restlessness. The best way to utilize this energy is to exercise. The feeling of well-being commonly experienced during or after exercise is due to the tranquilizing effect of endorphins, which are secreted by the brain. These are morphinelike substances, without any side effects.

Let's also understand that anger isn't in our nature. As soon as you feel angry, be aware of it, hold your breath, and start breathing deeply and consciously. This allows us to stand back and become a witness (*sakshi* in Sanskrit). When you watch from your Higher Self, you'll see that the agitation and disturbance lies on the surface. In this way, anger will dissolve and you'll realize that you're physically relaxed, emotionally calm, mentally alert, and spiritually aware . . . and that this is the *real* you. This blissful state can be your constant companion if you meditate on a regular basis.

🐚 🐚 🐚

I'd like to end this chapter with a story about Buddha's life.

Buddha was walking along with Ananda (his cousin and lifetime disciple) and a few of his other disciples when four or five young men stopped him and started showering him with abuse. Buddha just stood there—this made the young men very angry, so they started shouting more abuse. Buddha still stood there, not reacting. One of the men shouted, "Why don't you answer? Why are you quiet? Have you got nothing to say?"

Buddha replied, "You have come a little too late. If you had come along ten years earlier, I would have reacted, but I'm no longer open to receiving what you're trying to give me. I'm in a hurry—people are waiting for me in the next village. If you have finished, may I go? I'll be coming back along this same route, so perhaps you can meet me again."

The men were puzzled. One of them said, "Please say something—anything you like."

Buddha said, "The people of the village I last visited gave me some sweets when I was leaving. I only accept things to eat when I'm hungry, and at the time, I was not hungry, so I gave the sweets back to them, with love and blessings, to be distributed among the people of the village. Neither have I accepted the abuse you wanted to give me. What will you do with it now? I suggest that you drop the abuse on your way back to your village, and take in its place my love and blessings."

If you trample over jasmine flowers, they forgive you with fragrance. Buddha did the same to the angry men. And in Chapter 1, Naciketas asked for the love and welfare of his father who, in a fit of fury, had given him away to death.

St. Francis summed it up best when he said, "Lord, grant that I may seek to comfort than be comforted. To love rather than be loved."

CHAPTER ELEVEN

THE
BATTLE of LIFE
IS ONE
OF
CONTRARY DESIRES

*When you have the right thoughts and right desires and say,
"Mountain, move from here," the mountain will move.*

— Jesus

EOPLE MISINTERPRET THE SCRIPTURES when they say
that we should be "free" from want. As a matter
of fact, we don't need to be free from want in
order to not be troubled by it.

Living among sense objects and being in constant contact with them, it's easy to be lured by desire after desire.
But the person who finds his own degree of satisfaction is
the one who finds real peace and happiness, which can
never be achieved in the search for constant gratification.

If your desires benefit the people around you, you'll
find inner peace and happiness, which nobody can snatch
away from you. Material wealth doesn't provide such
peace of mind, because it isn't everlasting.

The teachings of the Bhagavad Gita and Upanishads, when properly understood, state that each one of us desires, but our desire should not disturb us. The right knowledge equals the right desires. And right desires lead to right actions, because they benefit the people around you—your family, the nation, and the world.

From the story of Naciketas, we learned that two paths lie in front of us: the path of the good, which gives you real satisfaction and joy; and the path of the pleasant, which gives you material wealth and transient pleasures. The choice you make depends on your desires.

Therefore, desire can be humans' greatest foe and also their greatest hope and friend. People who are selfish and have insatiable appetites are compared with fire: The more we feed such desire, the more its appetite increases and, ultimately, the person who desires is consumed.

🐚 🐚 🐚

In the great epic, *Mahabharta*, Krishna (representing our consciousness) doesn't fight the battle for his devotee and friend, Arjuna (who represents our mind), he only guides him. The message is that we have to fight our own life battles after seeking His guidance on how to tread the path of dharma, and not succumb to selfish desires.

Desire is nothing but a need you want fulfilled. If you suppress desire, it becomes guilt, but once you're rooted in the Higher Self, all desires encourage you to act in God. Such longings will result in selfless actions of love, compassion, service, and wealth. How can a sage of self-knowledge entertain desire for anything else?

On the other hand, when we walk down the ladder of evolution, the individual embodied soul forgets it isn't a wave and thinks it's the ocean itself, identifying with the body and the ego. As such, it circles the alluring world of objects and identifies itself with egotistic pursuits or emotions such as pride, success, worldly rewards, wealth, position, honor, and fulfillment of physical desires. Sometimes divinity is left behind and forgotten altogether, and human beings become terrorists and tyrants, killing innocent fellow beings for the sake of their own glory, power, or belief, ultimately becoming devil-like. Hitler and Pol Pot are examples of such selfish tyrants.

What is the solution to such problems in an age when the divisive forces constantly threaten peace and harmony in our society? If the embodied soul remains closer to its source instead of drifting away to ego gratification and sense objects, then qualities such as compassion, tolerance, forgiveness, honesty, trust, love, and service automatically come to the fore. Spirituality can bring people together because it takes us back to where we originate.

Give up whatever stands in the way of your "spiritual" pursuits. The biggest obstacle is ego—let go of it once and for all, and don't identify yourself with it. A human's usual attitude can be likened to a stag that's proud of its horns and admires its reflection in the water. But upon hearing the roar of an approaching tiger, it runs away— only to get its horns caught in the bushes.

The quest for a spiritual life is an evolutionary urge in all human beings. If your relationship to life is materialistic (name, fame, acquisition), you may feel incomplete and wanting. If you have a "spiritual" impulse, then you'll be called to a life that's more whole, complete, and fulfilled. You'll also feel at one with absolute truth and the Higher Self. Remember, you're free to choose the path *you* desire.

Desires are met through intention. Intention lays the groundwork for desire to manifest from the unmanifest. The only caveat is that you use your intent for the benefit of humankind, but this happens spontaneously when you're in alignment with the laws of nature.

Paramhansa Sri Rama Krishna said, "The breeze of His grace is always blowing; you only have to raise your sails to catch it." By "raising the sails," he apparently meant having the right desire. *At*tention energizes, *in*tention organizes its fulfillment.

In my own life, I had a great desire to be a teacher of medical education. It wasn't a selfish desire, and my intent drew me closer to its end. But imagine my great surprise and delight when my sons Deepak and Sanjiv also went on to become teachers in their respective fields.

My "right" desire set in motion great fulfillment. When you have love in your heart, magic happens, and your dreams come true. Mine certainly did.

CHAPTER TWELVE

REACHING THE SHORES

OF

IMMORTALITY

BY

CONQUERING

LIFE AND DEATH

We come, we go, and in between, we try to understand.

— Rod Steiger

FROM THE STORY OF NACIKETAS, we learned that Vajasravasa, his father, was mortally afraid of death. He knew he had to perish one day, but if he had to die, he had to also attain heaven. Everybody wants to go to heaven, but nobody wants to die. One of life's major fears is death, but in the ancient scriptures, death is not nearly so foreboding.

🐚 🐚 🐚

Mark Twain once remarked that although he knew that everybody had to die one day, he always felt that he might be the exception. Deep down, many people share

Mark Twain's feeling of "it can't happen to me." Facing up to the inevitability of death is a necessary task in old age. The reaction is somewhat like that of a terminally ill patient. The concerned person suffers from depression, a sort of anticipatory self-mourning, but during their final hours, a significant number are free from depression. They become quite expectant (though not happy) about death, and are ready for it.

Buddha taught his disciples (including Ananda), that those who had a self-disciplined life and who paid particular attention to love, compassion, selfless service, hope, joy, and interdependence led a life of dharma. Old age and disease didn't interfere with their lives, and death did not shake them.

Ananda broke down when he noticed that death was upon the blessed one. He also noticed that Buddha was a picture of tranquility, and his body was radiant and golden. Buddha said to Ananda, "This body is not me. Anybody who leads a life of dharma is a Buddha. He is as infinite as the sky."

Buddha, a symbol of austerity, love, and altruism, addressed for the last time everyone who had gathered around to pay him their last respects, saying, "All created things must pass away. Strive diligently for a life dedicated to right effort, one founded on recognition of sacred inviolability." His message is a message of life—of life here and now at this very moment. As for the metaphysical question of whether a human lives after death, Buddha was silent. He might as well have said, "We don't know whether a person *is* the body or is *in* the body while he is alive—how can we say after the death of their body that they are dead?"

The Zen masters also say that life and death are the deepest mysteries and may even be two aspects of the same mystery. The word *death* can be likened to a door—we don't know where it leads after it has been opened. We can see the door but not behind it. Why worry about what happens after you pass through the door? Why worry about the future? It's life in the *present moment* that's precious. If you live an active, intense life, you die in peace. If you drag your life, complaining all the time, you drag your death, also. Death is not a problem . . . but the living dead is.

Zen masters also say that death is not for those rooted at the center of their being—the cyclone is only on the periphery; it never reaches the center. A person who is rooted at the center of their being is fearless. He's not unafraid or brave—he is simply fearless. A brave person is one who has fear but goes against it, and a coward is one who has fear but goes with it. A wise person is neither; he is simply fearless. He just knows that death is a myth, a lie. For a wise person, death does not exist; only life or God exists. The moment you feel deathlessness, you feel the very source of life. A story from the ancient "Puranas" illustrates this beautifully.

An angry bear in the forest is chasing a traveler. To escape from the wild animal, the traveler dives into a dry well, but sees at its bottom a dragon with its jaws wide open ready to swallow him up. Not daring to climb out, the traveler grabs hold of a twig growing in a crack in the wall of the well and clings to it. Gradually, his hands become weaker. Then he sees two mice moving around the stem of the twig, beginning to chew at it. As the mice gnaw, the traveler notices a few drops of honey on the leaves of the twig, and he longs to lick the honey with his tongue. He has no fear of death.

🐚 🐚 🐚

We want to know what happens after death so we can get over our morbid fear of it. Imagine, if death were not present, no plant would have withered, no petals would have fallen off any flower, no animals or birds or humans would have perished. The whole world would be stagnant.

Einstein's Theory of Relativity rules out the idea that matter and energy were somehow "added" to space and time. Instead, they're all treated as showing a single totality. They're all different manifestations of a single continuity that extends through all events—past, present, and future.

The continuing totality of events is called the space and time continuum. As we move and travel through it, we get a partial and changing view of a few small, local events. It seems that birth and death are local events on the continuum. Wherever matter appears, the continuum itself is curved, and its geometry becomes complicated, giving the appearance of movement accelerated by force.

Einstein's approach is that reality is essentially invariant and indefinite, and the way to truth is a search for unity, which is beyond the disjointed appearances of our often limited world perceptions.

As Einstein said, "Nature holds her secrets because of her essential loftiness, but not by means of ruse." After all, wherever we find uncertainty, it shows our ignorance, and our ignorance shows unreality. Einstein refused to shut the door on deeper knowledge. There were difficulties associated with his work on the Unified Field Theory, which would go on to include forces other than gravitation. No other breakthrough was in sight. His real interest was in the underlying truth. In his later years, he said, "One thing I have learned in a long life is that all science measured against reality is primitive and childlike, and yet it is the most precious thing we have."

When we talk of death, we talk of the death of the physical body. The Creator wanted it that way because He intended to release Earth of the intolerable burden of an ever-growing population. Death of the body is inevitable and will come to the poor, the rich, the ignorant, and the enlightened. But we must realize that the physical dissolution of the body alone is not death—that's only a space and time event in the continuum of life. The real you, the embodied soul, will never die.

Greed, anger, lust, jealousy, ill will toward others, and lack of contentment are all slow poisons that you feed your body day after day, and your body is ultimately devoured by them. You also contribute to your own premature death by doing the wrong things, eating the wrong foods, and basking in negative emotions. Death comes from the confusion of perception—when we perceive truth, death cannot touch us. We're on the path of deathlessness, the path of immortality.

🐚 🐚 🐚

The near death experience (NDE) has been explained by people who have come back within a few minutes of apparently dying. It's said to be an altered state of consciousness that involves a feeling of timelessness, and complete freedom from pain and bliss. Researchers working in the field are of the opinion that this feeling of bliss and peace may be due to a blockage of the brain receptors to certain neurotransmitters that cause pain and misery. The NDE brings on conditions such as low blood flow, low oxygen levels, and temporal lobe hypoxia. If prolonged, it leads to brain death. If the NDE is a blissful experience, then wouldn't death itself be blissful?

Unfortunately, with the help of modern technology, patients who have reached the end of life and who are in great pain and misery are kept alive for months. The dying person isn't allowed to depart with dignity. We should realize that death is *not* a morbid event, and one should be able to age and die gracefully.

Take this next story, for example. When I first met Dr. Dabur, a busy and popular general practitioner, he was already in his mid-80s. He was a noble soul, and his patients loved him for his affectionate smile and his dedication to his work. He was admitted to our hospital with chest pain. He had unstable angina, and on his second day in the hospital, he had a severe heart attack. Dr. Dabur's face was peaceful and unperturbed. Even though he must have been in severe pain, he was calm, mentally alert, and clear.

He said to me, "I'm grateful to you for what you have done for me, and for what you want to do, but please don't disturb me any longer. I have had some good innings, and now I am going. I'm at the feet of the Lord—it's very peaceful here and I am in bliss. God bless you all."

The ECG monitor showed a straight line—his heart had stopped. I have seen many patients die in the hospital, but nothing like this. Each one of us in that room simply stood there in silence.

PART IV

THE
ELIXIR of LOVE:
THE
ONLY WEALTH
WORTH HAVING
IN
LIFE

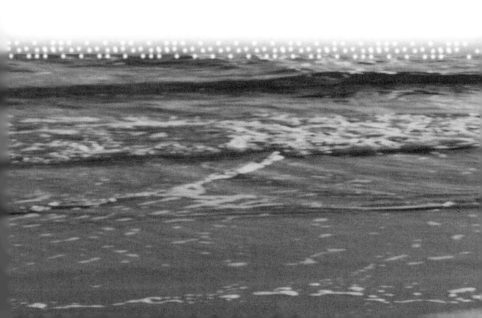

CHAPTER THIRTEEN

THE

SPIRIT

OF

LOVE

Communion with God is true wine, the wine of ecstatic love.

— Paramhansa Sri Rama Krishna

KAMA, THE GOD OF LOVE, is also the god of desire, and some ascetics see him as the love demon who brings on suffering if love is unfulfilled. In the Bhagavad Purana, an Indian mythological text, it's mentioned that Kama may lead to maddening passions, opening the door to lust: for sex, power, and battle. This only happens when the ego takes over and dominates the needs of the soul. Once that happens, Lord Shiva, the god of destruction, burns Kama to death by opening his third eye, the eye of discrimination. Is the love god gone? Not quite.

The gods approach Vishnu, the god of preservation, and with his grace, Krishna, who represents reality and consciousness, becomes the divine love god, and Kama becomes the love god of passionate romance with the divine.

🐚 🐚 🐚

The origin of love resides at the level of the Higher Self, the Creator, God. His force attracts, operates, and creates. Because God pervades everything, love operates at *all* levels of creation: Love draws particles of matter together. Birds and animals care for their little ones, and apparently love them until they grow up—usually it's instinctive and not very long-lasting. Love seems to be more abiding and meaningful among species such as elephants, dolphins, and gorillas, who have bigger, more developed brains. These animals express compassion, sorrow, and joy.

Some people prefer to call animal love a "bond." But a bond is a force of attraction and creation, so why not call it *love?* In animals, love is creative—in the sense that it continues the progeny of the species concerned in accordance with the dictates of the genes (DNA and RNA)—but it stops short. Love among animals simply means following what their genes dictate—it's responsible for the survival of their species. Through love, animals are attracted to their mates at particular times of the year—they sense pleasure in mating and begetting offspring.

A large number of human beings also stop short when it comes to love—their love culminates in the propagation of their progeny. In addition to, or instead of, reproductive love, many humans seek joy of the mind and intellect; and create art, poetry, and philosophy. If they seek joy at the level of Spirit, they're drawn to God and often experience ecstasy, achieving God-consciousness.

Human love is apparent between parents and children, husband and wife, and friends. And it can extend further to include the whole world, which is really one family *(vasudeva kutambam)*. This understanding helps us achieve immortality—parents through their offspring, and poets, artists, and philosophers through their poetry, art, or philosophy.

Love based on physical attraction alone is short-lived, ephemeral, transient, and unsatisfactory, but if there's an intellectual attraction or a deep friendship in addition to physical attraction, the bond is much stronger. Furthermore, if you move beyond that and glimpse the Higher Self, your love will be immortal. It's then that you love someone not merely for beauty and intelligence, but for who they really are. Human love becomes supreme when you see the divine in your beloved. You're then saturated with love—by living in bliss, you become love.

Think about this: When you see a sunset at the beach, you love it and don't expect anything in return for that love. When you express human love in the same way, you don't love someone for reward or fear of punishment. Love knows no fear; in fact, it actually *conquers* all fear.

But as long as there is ego—"I" and "me"—there's no room for love. When there *is* love in your heart, there can be no ego. When you meet a friend after a long time, there is joy and peace; there is no "I" or "me," only "we," the connected oneness, which is beyond ego. You fly on wings of love to your Higher Self, the divinity in you. It's during that union with the Higher Self that everything else is forgotten and only bliss remains. You've renounced ego, and the lower self (greed, lust, anger, and jealousy) is automatically renounced.

The entire universe is God manifesting in a multitude of names and forms. When you love God, you love the entire universe—everything and everybody in the universe—and when you love the universe, you love God.

Love for, and service to, your fellow beings is the best way to reach God—service is love in action. In love, one expands; and in fear, one shrinks. In love, you're open; in fear, you shut your doors. In love, you're never alone or lonely; you're not only connected with your beloved, but with all trees, forests, birds, the stars, the moon, the galaxies, the whole universe. It's only in fear that you're by yourself, a lonely, God-forsaken individual.

Out of love . . . truth, honesty, and trust are born. If you hold these values, then you're not afraid of anything or anybody. You have a sense of security that leads to the development of compassion, charity, generosity, devotion, dedication, discipline, gratitude, contentment, humility, the ability to forgive and forget and speak softly. If you're in touch with these values, you have inner peace and you overflow with joy, which has nothing to do with material possessions. Happy molecules rush through your body, and God's grace is there with you.

🐚 🐚 🐚

A man I've known for 45 years, Mr. Rattan, loves to play tennis. I'm amazed at and intrigued by his love for the game. He's 75 years old and riddled with arthritis, but as soon as he's on the court, he comes alive and plays a superb game for up to two hours.

I couldn't understand the phenomenon of Rattan's game of tennis. "Don't you get fed up playing tennis every day, day after day?" I asked him once.

"No, not at all," he replied. "It's great fun! It's the game that matters, and you know I love tennis with all my heart. I've heard that if you live in your heart, magic happens."

Rattan doesn't meditate regularly, but he does sit silently every morning and look out into nature—this has probably influenced every aspect of his life. It's something like Zen, the Japanese form of Buddhist meditation. Zen differs from other forms of Buddhism, holding that the mind should be left alone to function in an integrated and spontaneous way. As such, it develops a virtue called *te*, by which it acquires spontaneity that remains unaffected by outward circumstances.

The Samurai, the warrior class of Japan, incorporated Zen into such activities as sword fighting, archery, wrestling, and judo. They believed that after the techniques of various arts (the craft) are mastered, they must be discarded. This act releases the ingenuity and creativity of the mind. The emphasis is always on inner life. You don't *strive* for an effect—and then a day comes when the arrow flies straight to its target, the sword's thrust is made without reflection, or the tennis racket hits the ball on its own, and you find yourself playing while in meditation, without any intention or desire.

To practice Zen means to realize one's existence from moment to moment. Life isn't disturbed by regrets of the past or daydreaming of the future. To live in the present and revel in the Higher Self is a state of ecstatic wonder. A strange feeling of well-being and peace overwhelms you. It's the action of doing without being self-conscious of doing, between "doing" the act and "being caught in" the action.

You don't need to be a Zen Buddhist to achieve such an end. Rattan, for instance, won many prizes in tennis during his lifetime, but he never did it for the name and fame, nor is it for anybody else that he continues to play today. He continues to live in magical simplicity, loving everyone around him, and he continues to play because he loves every moment of the game and isn't interested in impressing anyone or showing off.

Just remember, "If you live in your heart, magic happens."

CHAPTER FOURTEEN

HUMAN LIFE IS

A

GIFT of LOVE

All knowledge is vain, save when there is work.
And all work is empty, save when there is love.

— Khalil Gibran

IN CHAPTER 9, I shared the story of Asthavakra with you. He was severely disabled, described as "being bent in eight places like a camel"—yet in spite of his handicap, he became a rishi (a great sage) and a philosopher. In the contemporary world, many individuals with physical or mental challenges have achieved great things as well.

For example, Helen Keller—blind and deaf from scarlet fever since she was 19 months old—not only learned to read, write, and speak, but also obtained a university degree, authored books, became a lecturer, and worked all her life for the physically disabled.

While she was studying at Radcliffe College, Keller wrote: "I fall, I stand still, I trudge, and I gain a little. . . . I become more eager and climb higher and begin to see the widening horizon. Every struggle is a victory."

Stephen Hawking, a brilliant, world-famous scientist, suffers from amyotrophic lateral sclerosis (ALS), a rare disease that handicaps movement and speech. Journalists have questioned him about his life—it's a fascinating story of a physically challenged genius with a paralyzed body and extraordinary mind who makes the most out of life by being active and creative.

"All my adult life," said Hawking, "I have been warned that I may have an early death, so I'm not afraid. But I am in no hurry to die; there is so much I want to do first."

When asked, "What keeps you going?" Hawking answered, "I thought at one time, *Why should this happen to me?* Then I realized many people are more unlucky than I am. Young, promising lives are cut short by accidents. When I was in the hospital once, I saw a boy in the bed opposite die of acute leukemia. It was certainly not nice to see. At least my condition didn't make me feel sick.

"After the diagnosis was made, I didn't know what was going to happen to me or how rapidly the disease would progress. My dreams were disturbed. How could I best utilize my life? There seemed to be a cloud hanging over my future for a while. However, I was not bothered about how long I was going to live as long as I could utilize my life the best way I knew how."

Stephen Hawking has reached the pinnacles of glory—even physically robust and intelligent people haven't been able to achieve what he has. Only those who love and enjoy their work are achievers. Swami Vivekananda said, "You should know that if you rest, you rust, and your fortune rests. If you sleep, it sleeps with you. It rises when you rise. Therefore, rise, shake off your laziness, and enjoy your work." You can only do that if you love your work.

If you love your work, then in due course, you don't work *for* joy, you work *from* joy, and you reach a point when all stumbling blocks become stepping-stones to success. Previously, you were set adrift along the stream of time, but you now know that you can swim in the right direction. Love for your work is divine—it comes from the creator, the Higher Self—and overflows to your fellow human beings.

🐚 🐚 🐚

In Chapter 1, we saw that Vajasravasa, Naciketas's father, organized a sacrificial feast called a Yajna. He announced that he was going to give everything he possessed to the priests, but Naciketas knew the truth.

It doesn't matter how grand and philanthropic your act looks, if it has a selfish motive, it's not charity. On the other hand, if your action is selfless and does good, it gives you inner joy and peace, especially if you don't entertain the idea that you're doing it for name and fame.

The Bhagavad Gita states that humans are bound to their actions *except* when they're performed for the sake of sacrifice and performed efficiently. When work is done in the spirit of sacrifice, there cannot be any bargaining. You don't offer something in sacrifice for the sake of gain. The final act of any sacrifice is renouncing the ego of "I" did it, "I" sacrificed. Once ego is placated, sacrifice promotes a feeling of peace and bliss.

Sacrifice is all around you: The sun shines to give you life, the moon appears to give you peace, the ocean sends you rain, and the earth provides you with food. Service and sacrifice follow the laws of nature. Those who work in the spirit of sacrifice attain Heaven while on Earth, and enjoy eternal peace and bliss, the greatest expression of human love.

CHAPTER FIFTEEN

THE
ART
OF
GIVING
IN
LOVE

He who gives liberally goes straight to the gods.
On the high ridge of heaven, he stands exalted.

— Rig Veda

PEOPLE GIVE ALL THE TIME without expectation. One such example was a young boy named Yong Rok Kim from South Korea. The Belmont Hill School in Boston awarded him the honor of best graduate, saying that he had distinguished himself in a number of ways, including his show of sensitivity toward others. His love and compassion for other children was unbounded, and whatever money he saved from his scholarship and earnings from odd jobs, he sent back home to South Korea for the poor children in his hometown. He didn't know these children—he knew they needed support, not pity, and he expected nothing in return. The gift of love from Kim to the children of South Korea was just purely given from his heart.

Giving a gift is not a transaction, and a gift should be given without a motive. A gift is contaminated if it's based on hunger for recognition, self-congratulatory arrogance—or if it's given as an act of patronage intended to buy one a place in society or history, or to bribe one's way to prestige. If a gift is tainted in such a way, it should be refused, because it disturbs the peace of both the giver *and* the recipient. Unless you give away part of what you've earned by hard work and through love, you can't get credit for it.

Mother Teresa was an apostle of love, peace, and altruism. Her life was spent serving the poor and downtrodden. She served not only the hungry, sick, and lonely—but even the dying were brought to her various charity homes, where they were clothed and fed. "Even if we cannot save them at this terminal stage," Mother Teresa said, "we can certainly help them die with dignity."

Mother Teresa saw God in everyone. She gave unconditional, unbounded love to all, along with the inspiration to serve lovingly. She was a legend in her lifetime, and people called her "the Saint of Calcutta."

Krishna states in the Bhagavad Gita that a gift given to the wrong person at the wrong time, not presented from the heart, or delivered in proud contempt, is a gift of darkness that brings disharmony to fellow beings. On the other hand, if you give great blessings unconditionally, your life itself becomes bliss and peace.

Therefore, it's the *intention* behind giving and receiving that is the most important thing. The intention should always be to create happiness. The act of giving has to be joyful, and the frame of mind has to be one in which you feel joy in the very act of giving. Then the energy behind the gift increases many times over. If you want joy, give joy to others. If you want love, learn to give love. If you want attention and appreciation, learn to give attention and appreciation. In fact, the easiest way to get what you want is to help others get what they want.

In her early life, Florence Nightingale (1820–1910) was blessed with every material advantage that an English life could offer, yet when she was only 16, she started to break free from the cocoon of her Victorian family life and decided to make nursing her vocation.

In 1854, during the Crimean War, she took a team of nurses to Scutari (now Turkey). After all of the other medical officers had retired for the night, this angel of mercy and altruism would be seen making her rounds alone throughout the night, night after night. She had a smile on her face, a lamp in her hand, and love in her heart. She dressed the wounds of the injured and the sick with an outpouring of love, and she brought them cheer. It was real love in action—which is selfless service to the needy—without the faintest desire for recognition. There were no antibiotics in those days, and surgical techniques weren't very sophisticated, yet the death rate among the wounded soldiers fell from 42 percent to 2 percent after Florence Nightingale arrived on the scene. Naturally, recognition came on its own accord, and Nightingale became one of the most respected and famous women in England at that time.

And the immortal lady of the lamp lives on. Her contributions to the evolution of the nursing profession were invaluable, including the opening of a school that marked the beginning of professional education in the field. Nursing care is responsible for saving millions of lives all over the world . . . and it all resulted from one remarkable woman's loving, unselfish acts.

CHAPTER SIXTEEN

APPEARING

TO

BE WHAT YOU

ARE NOT

You have to be. You cannot be this, you cannot be that.

— Raman Maharishi

O NCE A SUFI SAINT WAS TRAVELING along with his disciples. During the journey, he camped near a large grove of trees upon which doves were perched. As they rested, one of the disciples aimed at one of the doves, killed it, cooked it, and then ate it. After that incident, a flock of doves came and hovered over the head of the Sufi saint, who was resting under one of the trees. The Sufi asked the leader of the flock what the matter was.

The leader replied, "We have a complaint to make against you. One of your disciples has killed one of us."

The Sufi called the disciple concerned and asked him what had happened. The disciple said he hadn't done any-thing wrong—he was hungry and had killed one of the birds to eat. The Sufi conveyed this to the leader of the birds.

The leader replied, "Perhaps you have failed to under-stand. What we're complaining about is that all of you came here in the garb of Sufis, yet acted as hunters. Had you come dressed as hunters, we would certainly have remained alert. When we saw you in the guise of Sufis, we thought we were safe and remained perched on top of the tree without being properly vigilant. You shouldn't appear to be what you are not."

♪ ♪ ♪

The fox is cunning by nature, the cat is a great hunter, and the dog is faithful . . . but humans are different. We have both "good" *and* "bad" qualities, and we can transcend both by virtue of our spiritual nature.

For those who desire liberation from the bondage of duality, truth must be practiced diligently. It's possible for all people to nurture truth in daily life. If our minds are pure, our speech will also be truthful—and we should always think before we speak because we can't take our words back.

When truth is strictly adhered to in daily life, the mind becomes discriminatory and pure, and naturally withdraws from wrongdoing. Like a splash of mud that shows glaringly on white clothes, a wrong action or untruth by a spiritually evolved person stands out. Diligence in life is essential for spiritual progress.

If you're traveling along the highway and come across a rugged shortcut, be careful you don't break the car's axles in the interest of saving time. For a creative and happy life, it's best to stay on the path of righteousness and truthfulness—even if it does take a little longer.

Some people believe that lies reduce social friction, and that a lie told firmly and bravely is romantic and noble. Bella De Paullo, a psychology professor at the University of Virginia, has found that in a ten-minute conversation, a fifth of the content is untruth, and this increases to a third of the conversation if the participants have been university educated. Education seems to give some people the vocabulary and confidence to get away with lies.

Falsehood (*asatya*) may appear advantageous at times, but ultimately, the victory is truth. Asatya may seem harmless when viewed superficially, but it forms the basis of fraud. And people who lie all the time have apparently not heard about the doctrine of karma. But even if they have, they don't seem to understand that nothing you think, say, or do is without a consequence—it's a cause-and-effect equation. These liars only believe that the world hates a loser who isn't materially or socially well off.

As the standard of living goes up, the quality of life goes down—there's more fraud, deception, corruption, bribery, late-night partying, and accumulation of wealth. Such people live in a sordid, tawdry world of their own, and all this drags the soul down to subhuman existence. Then they throw a mountain of negative karma into the bargain, which returns what they put out into the universe right back to them without fail . . . and there is no escape. Everybody has to pay their karmic debt, whether it's in this life or the one hereafter. The cosmic computer keeps account.

It's only through simplicity; plain speaking; and adhering to truth, humility, compassion, and serenity that you'll be allowed to attune with the Higher Self. The liars, the vain, the greedy, and the deceitful will never be able to achieve peace of mind. Ultimate victory is that of truth.

🜪 🜪 🜪

In the great Indian mythological epic, *Mahabharta,*
Krishna prompted Yudishtra, the apostle of justice and
truth, to tell a lie. Why would Krishna do that? Because
he realized that Drona, a great teacher of warfare and master of using various lethal weapons, was on the side of evil
and had a secret in his possession. When he started using
this deadly weapon, the army of the Pandavas started to
fall, and thousands of men died instantly. It was an unjust
war, and Krishna could see that unless Drona was made
to lay down his arms, there would be no soldier left in the
Pandavas army.

Krishna called on Yudishtra to help, and after he related
his plan, Yudishtra agreed to tell a lie, the first of his life.

Yudishtra told Drona, "Ashwathama, the elephant, is
dead." Ashwathama was the name of an elephant that had
been killed a short time ago; it was also the name of
Drona's brave and only son. It's said that Yudishtra said
the word *Ashwathama* loudly, but the word *elephant* in
a low tone so that Drona wouldn't hear it.

(Another version of the story is slightly different.
According to this version, Krishna asked Bhima, one of
the Pandavas brothers, to shout that Ashwathama was
killed. When he did so, Drona was not flustered because
he knew Bhima wasn't a truthful man. Krishna then told
Yudishtra to repeat the same statement, but he refused
because he would never resort to a falsehood. Then the
elephant Ashwathama was killed and Yudhistra was
asked to announce the death. Krishna then blew the
conch at such a time that Yudhistra's words "The elephant
named Ashwathama has been killed" were heard by
Drona as "Ashwathama has been killed.")

Drona was grief-stricken because he knew Yudhistra
would never tell a lie. The strategy was appropriately

advantageous and practical. Drona, who was behaving like a devil, was soon killed, and thousands and thousands of lives were saved.

Nevertheless, Yudhistra's chariot, which was said to always ride four inches above the ground due to the inner strength of Yudhistra's truth, began to crawl.

❧ ❧ ❧

In practice, the pursuit of any ideal is bound to have doubts and obstacles. Upholding truth in life has been hailed in the scriptures as capable of bestowing the highest good, which is liberation. Philosophically, there are three levels of truth: the absolute truth (God); empirical truth (perceiving the sky as blue although it isn't); and apparent truth (a mirage seen in the desert).

Speaking the truth in day-to-day life is only one facet of truth—the more profound aspect of its practice is to be true to one's conscience in thought, word, and deed. Truthful speech shouldn't be elusive, misleading, or meaningless. For example, truth for the sake of speaking the truth, but which hurts others, is not truth. Even if it has to be told, it should be told in such a manner that it's pleasant to the listener. In day-to-day life, it's not always practical to do this; therefore, one should speak with discretion. Physicians who are supposed to heal patients with comforting words should be especially careful with this.

For example, one of our patients, a lady of 75, had been under treatment for diabetes and a heart ailment for many years. Sometime into her treatment, she was found to have Hodgkin's disease. In view of her heart condition and the possible side effects of chemotherapy, and in consultation with her family, it was decided not to tell the patient what she had. She lived comfortably for six years after that, and treatment for her heart was continued. The outcome may have been completely different if she'd been told the absolute truth.

It's important to have knowledge of what is real, what our fundamental nature is, and the absolute truth. The knowledge of absolute truth can also be referred to as the knowledge of the true nature of the Higher Self. In fact, truth can be described as the primary purpose of life and the basis of all other human values. Truth is the ultimate value of human freedom. Those who love and observe truth love the Creator, God, and are real seekers of the Higher Self—they don't accept anything less.

CHAPTER SEVENTEEN

THE TAJ MAHAL:
A LOVE SONG IN MARBLE,
OR A
SYMBOL
OF
SHAH JAHAN'S
SELF-GLORIFICATION?

Knowing the eternal means enlightenment.
Not knowing the eternal causes passion
to arise and that is evil.

— Lao Tse

IN 1631, SHAH JAHAN, EMPEROR OF INDIA, sat at the bedside of his beloved queen, Mumtaz Mahal, who died while giving birth to the last of the 14 children she bore the emperor during their 19 years of marriage. After her death, the emperor cancelled all appointments, went to his rooms, and bolted the doors from the inside. For eight days, he stayed there without food or wine, and the only sound that came from his rooms was a low, continual moan.

When he finally emerged, his hair had turned gray and his back was bent. He ordered his entire country to be in official mourning: All popular music and public amusement activities were banned; and perfumes, cosmetics, jewelry, and brightly colored clothes were forbidden. Any offenders were charged with showing disrespect to the late queen and punished. He changed his royal cape for white robes, and soon all of the country was dressed in white. Shah Jahan professed such intense love for Mumtaz Mahal that people thought he wasn't going to live long after her death. For two long years, he mourned her.

Before her death, Mumtaz Mahal had whispered a final wish in the emperor's ear: She asked that he build a monument of eternal wonder to celebrate their love. Soon after her death, construction on the Taj Mahal began. Ustad Isa, the architect of the Taj Mahal, employed 20,000 workers and took 20 years to complete the mausoleum. Today, it stands as one of the greatest marvels of the world—an exquisite and beautiful memorial of the love between Mumtaz Mahal and Shah Jahan, who lie in tombs at the very heart of the grounds.

In the Taj Mahal, the rich tapestry of visual images— carved, painted, and bejeweled with semiprecious stones— along with verses from the holy Koran, transport the visitor to a different world. The "white jewel" is the most resplendent monument ever built by a man for the woman he loved. It continues to reflect the glory of the emperor's love for his queen—but was this love divine?

Many people don't know that the savage in Shah Jahan was very strong. He ordered the killing of Khan-e-Jahan Lodi, which was generally accepted, since Khan-e-Jahan was a rebel. But the emperor also sent an order that Hassan, the captive son of Khan-e-Jahan, be disposed of so he didn't

THE TAJ MAHAL . . .

"pollute the fair air of this country with his foul breath." The emperor's command was carried out, and Hassan was put to death by hammering red-hot iron rods through his head.

The way Shah Jahan came to power also shows a ruthless nature. He murdered his brother and "cleansed" the army of any disloyal elements, killing thousands of men. Any person who has unconditional love in his heart for his beloved has a glimpse of the divine and love for all creation. He can never be as cruel as Shah Jahan was.

There's no doubt that Shah Jahan had an eye for fine art, architecture, and music, and created the Taj Mahal, a wonder of wonders, for Mumtaz Mahal—but historical accounts show that the savage dominated the lover in him, and he was certainly no puritan.

(The story of the great emperor's official mourning at the beginning of this chapter seems to originate from the *Padsha Nama*, the royal gazette, and may therefore suggest bias.)

🐚 🐚 🐚

Based on what Chung Tzu (365–290 B.C.), Chinese Taoist master and philosopher, said about truth, love, and purity, one who puts on a show of lamenting and sadness evokes no sympathy or grief. He who forces himself to be angry may sound fierce but will arouse no awe; and he who forces himself to be affectionate, though he may smile, will create no air of warmth or love.

True sadness makes no sound, true anger doesn't have to show itself to arouse awe, and true love needn't smile to create warmth. When a man has love in his heart and truth within himself, the vibrations of love flow to all living beings to bring peace and harmony.

Love is a creative force. Shah Jahan loved Mumtaz Mahal, but he was also vain and loved himself. Nevertheless, Mumtaz Mahal inspired her lover, and it was the magic of her love that transformed Shah Jahan and gave the Taj Mahal to the world. The Taj Mahal will always remind us that love does indeed conquer all.

CHAPTER EIGHTEEN

LOVE APPEARS

IN

MANY GUISES

Thou soul of my soul. I shall clasp thee again.

— Robert Browning

I'D LIKE TO END THIS BOOK by looking at examples of the different kinds of love that exist among humans here on Earth.

Heavenly Love

Love is for all times and all seasons, and so are the love songs of Rabindra Nath Tagore. Tagore covered every aspect of love in his songs and stories, and drew inspiration from varied sources. Love flows in an endless stream through his words, which include more than 1,000 poems and 2,000 songs, in addition to a large number of short stories, novels, and plays. When he was 70, Tagore took to painting and produced 3,000 extraordinary works. He made contributions to education and social reform, and it was his profound love for nature and beauty that inspired him and is reflected in all his work.

Kadambri Devi, his sister-in-law, was the focal point of his attention. She died young, but there was something in her that haunted Tagore, and his impressions of her were reflected in his poems and stories. His relationship with Victoria Ocampo, an Argentinian advocate of women's rights and equality of the sexes, inspired Tagore to write the book of verse called *Purvi*. Tagore's love for Kadambri and Victoria Ocampo was based upon intellectual attraction. It was this enduring, inspirational love—a glimpse of the Higher Self—that led him to create immortal poetry, music, and art.

Tagore once wrote to Ocampo, "I trust my providence. I say . . . in all humility, that God has chosen me for a special mission and . . . I believe that your love may in some way help me to my fulfillment." Tagore trusted in love and was aware that the ego can stand in the way of progress to spiritual freedom. His work allows us to share in his divine understanding of love and life so that we may glimpse heaven, too.

Amorous Love

Kalidasa was a poet who appreciated the beauty, romance, and enjoyment of life. His imaginative description of human form, beauty, and love was second to none—but Kalidasa also stated in his work that unregulated sensual love leads to madness. He felt that since love is a vital cosmic force, it shouldn't be confined to sensual pleasure.

Kalidasa was a great naturalist. He was sensitive to the changes that occurred in the spring, and related them to human mood and passion. The response of human beings to this season is fascinating. Although humans make love and mate throughout the year (unlike plants and animals), the tendency to make love is heightened in the spring. The poets have linked spring weather with Kama, the god of love and desire.

Kalidasa's famous poem "Kumara Sambhava" describes how spring descends upon Earth and creates an entrancing, intoxicating atmosphere suited to amorous passion. Kama's arrows and the effects of spring shake the equilibrium of even the most divine mind and charge it with passion.

The pigment in plants called *phytochrome* senses the length of the day. When the day's length increases, as it does in spring, plants start to flower. Birds lay eggs and most animals deliver their young in spring, when plants are flowering. Even the elephant delivers in spring, after 645 days of gestation. With a well-defined reproductive cycle, there are switches that turn the male and female elephant on for the grand act of mating. It's believed that when an elephant goes into "muskch," it heralds its readiness for mating.

Several centuries ago, the poet Neelakanta wrote of the muskch condition: It brings about excitement, swiftness, order, love, passion, complete fluorescence of the body, wrath, prowess, and fearlessness.

There are two special glands called temporal glands on each side of the head of the elephant where a discharge occurs. Muskch (the word is derived from *musk*) is the odor that attracts elephants to mate. When a male elephant comes into muskch, its physiology and behavior change dramatically: The level of the male sex hormone testosterone rises, increasing its aggression and desire for mating.

Whether the muskch fluid has a special odor or a sexual "come hither" signal for the female is yet to be established. Dr. Bala Subramanium, an eminent molecular biologist, explains that similar sex scents are released by many species and are referred to as *pheromones* (from the Greek *phero,* meaning "convey"; and *mone,* coming from *hormone*). Pheromones can attract or repel members of the opposite sex.

The mechanism behind this phenomenon is little understood at present. Dr. Subramanium notes that pheromones may be present in birds, reptiles, lower mammals, and human beings, where they're suppressed now and again, reappearing at different times throughout evolution. To date, Dr. Subramanium says that no pheromone molecules have been found in human beings, but I feel that they must be there.

Say, for example, you enter a room to meet a person you've never met before. You hit it off right away, and soon after, you become friends. I put it down to pheromones attracting (or repelling if you feel put off by the same person). Pheromones are likely to be subtle, and as yet, we're unable to isolate the molecules, but they still may be what is responsible for the force of attraction that joins friends, parents to their children, or a man to a woman.

It's the physical, biological, amorous level of love that draws us near—yet many other factors help to sustain it to the point where we move beyond physical love to the intellectual and the spiritual.

Instinctive Love

A bull's only purpose in life seems to be to grow to maturity and reproduce in order to propagate the species. The cow looks after the calf, and has compassion for the offspring for some time . . . and then forgets all about them. Birds sing to announce that they're ready for mating and build nests. They look after their little ones after the eggs have hatched, then the little ones fly away—and the parents forget about them and fly to another place.

Human beings also have an instinctive urge to propagate, but there's much more to sex than what first meets the eye. After all, for human beings, it's more important for love to be associated with courtship and the sacred bonds of marriage. The affection and love between well-matched couples moves beyond materialistic needs and barriers. Mating then becomes a sacred act based on true love, resulting in ecstasy.

Love Turned Sour

It's important to quickly mention the other types of human love, too—such as unrequited and obsessive love. These types of love are usually based in fear and insecurity, the need to control, or the desire to experience pain. This kind of love gives love a bad name. As a simple example, obsessive love deprived the world of John Lennon's soul-stirring music. Beware of falling into this type of love.

Savage Love

On the one hand, there is "I will give up everything" love—such as the love between King Edward VIII and Mrs. Wallis Simpson—and on the other hand, there is savage love.

In a recent debate on love between some members of the elite society of Delhi, India, different views were expressed. Some participants opined that the "urge to merge" was being equated with "true love." One of the female participants said that a number of women feel that, whether they like it or not, they have to yield to their husbands' demand for sex to keep the marriage going, for when a woman doesn't give in, love burns out. This certainly should *not* be the story of love after marriage.

Even outside of marriage, the modern love story isn't the romantic love story of yesteryear. In fact, the teenage lovers of today aren't virginal flowers or romantic innocents. They're roaring tigers at heart who have a devouring hunger to merge, after which the so-called love fades, or may continue as lust. And lust, whether for sex, money, or power, ultimately leads to destruction. By allowing lust to rule and the body to dominate the mind and intellect, human beings have given a different meaning to the power of sex.

It says in the Bhagavad Gita that lust, greed, and anger are the triple gates to hell. Only by showing that sex is more than just a physical exercise—by putting it to its best and legitimate use—can humans justify their existence.

Since the beginning of time, lust has been mentioned at the top of the list of negative human attributes. The response of humans to lust and infidelity has been the same in all societies, regardless of creed and culture. But let it be known that such attributes drag you down the ladder of evolution. It's the experience of divine love that lifts you up.

Divine Love

According to a nationwide opinion poll held in Britain in October 1997, the greatest love poem in English history is Elizabeth Barrett Browning's "How Do I Love Thee?" Not only is this poem a remarkable piece of literature, it came from the depth of Elizabeth's heart and soul. And behind this poem is one of the greatest *true* love stories of the world.

Elizabeth Barrett's possessive and authoritarian father, an English country gentleman named Edward Mautten Barrett, was more fond of her than his other 11 children because she was very pretty and started writing poetry at an early age.

At 15, a fall from a horse shattered Elizabeth's nerves, and when she was 22, her mother died. By then, she was in poor health and confined to her room, suspected to be suffering from consumption (tuberculosis). Her illness worsened when her brother Edward, whom she loved very much, drowned while swimming in the sea.

Elizabeth spent her days cooped up in her room, resting and writing; consequently, she poured out creative poetry (albeit with a somewhat melancholy tone) from her sad heart. Before long, she became a well-known poet, with several published volumes under her belt. Yet she was miserable because there was no hope of escape from her prison—which consisted of her illness, her one room, and her father's tyrannical rule.

Her father's cousin, John Kenyen, brought Elizabeth news of the stimulating life in London. In his talks, one poet figured prominently: His name was Robert Browning, and he had already made a name for himself as a poet. Elizabeth and John Kenyen admired his poems, and she had one of his portraits framed and hung on the wall of her room, along with those of four other highly regarded poets.

Robert Browning was in Italy when one of his poems was printed in Elizabeth's collected works, which appeared in two volumes. Poetry requires imagination and the ability to express the same in appropriate words and manner— Elizabeth's ability to do so was superb. Returning to England in December 1844, Robert picked up the volume and was delighted to find Elizabeth's flattering remarks about his own poetry.

Robert had enjoyed Elizabeth's poems very much and had heard about her from John Kenyen. Robert wrote to Elizabeth about the excellence of her poetry—its fresh, strange music; and true, brave new thoughts. So began one of the most fascinating correspondences in English literature, and an equally captivating story of divine love.

Letters of admiration flowed between Elizabeth Barrett and Robert Browning. Robert repeatedly begged her to allow him to visit. Elizabeth longed to meet him, but was afraid to face the moment and kept putting it off. She wrote, "Winters shut me up as they do dormouse's eyes. In the spring, we shall see."

Quickly, Robert replied with cheer and optimism, "I will joyfully wait for the delight of your friendship and the spring."

Elizabeth felt insecure, not only because of her illness, but also because she was six years older than Browning and had little world experience. But finally, the invitation was sent, and Robert and Elizabeth met. He was immediately struck by the beauty of her eyes. He stayed for an hour and a half, although later she confessed to him that "when you came, you never went away." The love was mutual, and during subsequent meetings, Robert poured out his love for Elizabeth.

At first, her father didn't think that there was anything between Elizabeth and Robert besides literary friendship. Soon, however, he started to resent Robert's growing influence on his daughter. Robert would help Elizabeth stand in the room and gently guide her to the window, where she could take in the beauty of the garden. He would also help her walk down the stairs to the living room. Elizabeth's health improved so much that she was able to go out in a carriage.

Robert's anguish was great as he watched Elizabeth's (and her siblings') helplessness under their father's tyranny. Elizabeth, however, knew that the choice had to be made between love and a life of imprisonment and death. On September 12, 1846, Elizabeth Barrett and Robert Browning were secretly married, and a week later, Elizabeth left her father's house forever. In a letter to her father, she pleaded, "Forgive me for the sake of the daughter you once loved." Her letters begging for forgiveness were subsequently sent back to her years later, unread and unopened.

To Robert, his wife was "lyric love." He was always intoxicated with the love he had for her. And to Elizabeth, Robert was everything. Elizabeth was an invalid when he first met her—although no definite diagnosis was ever made, her disability was very real to her—and she often felt that she was a picture of helpless indolence.

Robert Browning's intense, unconditional, unbounded love and devotion to Elizabeth made her life beautiful, more creative, and fulfilled. Their divine love transcended superficial feelings and reactions. It was divine love. They shared the magic of true unconditional love, which each of them sought subconsciously. Remember . . . whatever you seek, you will find.

Divine Love Is True Love

You see a sunset on the beach, the stars and the moon in the sky, flowers in bloom, the forests, or snow-peaked mountains—and you love each of them because they are glorious signs of beauty. It's a partial appreciation of divine beauty, supreme consciousness, the Lord himself. He illuminates everything in the universe. He shines; everything shines.

There is a spark of this divine love and bliss in any attraction between two human beings. One of the names of the Lord is *Hari*, which means "the one who attracts." It also means one who removes all obstructions and distractions—the one who heals you and the world.

When you're fascinated by the beautiful smile of your beloved, you aren't attracted to the atoms and molecules that make that smile. No, behind the particles is the play of divine love. You love a child because you love the Lord—you may not see Him, but he's there, beckoning and attracting you. Fire always leaps upward because it wants to meet with its source, the sun. Water always flows down toward its source, the ocean. Similarly, you love the Lord, your source, and desire to be at one with Him, who is within you. When you're in love with the Lord and have great attachment to Him, you don't have to renounce anything, for no worldly object can hold you now. When a person is in love, anything and everything that belongs to their beloved is very dear and even sacred to them because they have had a glimpse of the divine. Love seeks nothing other than itself—it's not only the means, it's also its own end.

🐚 🐚 🐚

Swami Vivekananda said that when a man attains love of God, he loves all and hates none, and is forever content. It's the same intense love that a nondiscriminating person has for the fleeting objects of the senses. But when love for God is fully developed, this love can't be exploited for health or wealth, for longevity or happiness. In it, there is no room for jealousy or hatred because the lover of God sees *everything* as God's manifestation. His devotion is the ideal of spiritual life and the means to attain it.

A true lover casts aside his isolation, arrogance, and ego, and when love is pure and the lover sees the divinity in his beloved, then the lover, the beloved, and God become one, and there is no possibility of separation.

Whenever there is true love in your heart, miracles happen. They may be in the form of poetry, fine arts, or music. You become more creative—the inspiration comes from the cosmos, and your perceptions become ever finer so that your eyes can see and your ears can hear what you didn't see or hear earlier.

EPILOGUE

PLANTS AND ANIMALS HAVE INTELLIGENT LIFE because they grow, multiply, and respond to external stimuli. Animals share "bonds" of love with their mates and offspring; however, they don't have the ability to realize what it means to be alive. Animals have no ego.

Humans are the only animals who are aware of themselves and aware of the awareness. People have the freedom to choose whether to be vegetarian or nonvegetarian. Human beings have no "time clock"—they have the choice to extend their life span to 90, 100, or 120 years. Although it's rare to reach 120, the choice is there.

Humans have an intellect and a sharp sense of discrimination. Humans are also restless, with a burning desire to know who they are, what the purpose of their life is, and what will happen to them after death. As we've journeyed together through this book, we've come across these questions—the mystery and magic of the origin of the universe and life has seemed interesting enough, although we couldn't really *solve* the mystery.

The Big Bang theory is similar to the ancient Indian theory of *manifestation of the universe*. According to some predictors and astrologers, the universe is likely to start contracting in the first decade or two of the 21st century, when our world will disintegrate and disappear. (There have been no scientific comments about this.) In any case, if this is so, we can't do anything about it, so why not enjoy life while the going is good?

What we really have to understand, regardless of what we believe, is that our day-to-day lives are influenced by two forces: (1) The first is the reality, the truth (or God) within and outside yourself, that operates through love, and is the greatest force of attraction. It also takes you to divinity and inspires innovative and creative acts such as art, poetry, and music. (2) The second force that can strongly influence people is the devil—who resides within you, me, and everyone—also known as the ego. The ego plays havoc with every one of us, unless a strict vigilance is kept over its activities. Never let the ego overwhelm you—in love, there is no "I," "me," or "mine."

The tussle in our lives is between the two vital forces—love and ego. This applies only to human beings because we are aware of our existence and our surroundings, and wish to explore the origin of the universe and life.

Humans are also free to decide what to do with their lives. They have the choice to have a *good time* or a *good life*. When ego dominates, a human being's sense of discrimination is clouded and ego takes them to the valley of ignorance, misery, and unhappiness through the corridors of greed, hatred, lust, anger, spite, and transient sensual pleasures.

If love dominates one's life, there's no room left for ego. Love takes you through the corridors of charity (the art of giving), compassion, dedication, humility, the ability to forgive and forget, contentment, and gratitude. Heaven on Earth is enjoyed, and the petty existence of jealousy and worry is replaced with a life of sunshine, peace, and bliss.

When love rules our thoughts, deeds, and actions, we enter the valley of eternal joy for the soul. Love for, and service to, your fellow human beings follows spontaneously, which is the best way to reach God. Love is the greatest human virtue—when it becomes divine, its fragrance constantly flows through you to all those around you, reaching far and wide.

GLOSSARY

Arjuna: The hero of the great epic *Mahabharta*. It was to him that Lord Krishna imparted the teachings of the Bhagavad Gita.

Asthavakra: The name literally means "bent in eight places." A sage at the age of 12, the dialogue between him and King Janaka forms the text of the ancient *Asthavakra Gita*.

Atman: The embodied soul. It is *sat*, *chit*, and *ananda* (existence, knowledge, and bliss). Atman is beyond the limitations of the body, mind, and intellect—beyond time and space.

Bhagavad Gita: The great ancient Indian scripture. The dialogue between Arjuna and Krishna represents an exchange between an embodied soul and the supersoul, the supreme consciousness. Krishna reveals the knowledge of life and living, and the path of dharma.

Brahman: Derived from the root *brh*, which means "to grow," *brahman* means "bigger than big." Biggest, when not associated with an object, indicates limitless. Brahman is the Higher Self, supreme consciousness.

Buddha: Comes from the root *bugh*, to be awake, to be conscious of, to know. In India, Gautama became Buddha after enlightenment.

Ego (*ahmkara*): The identification of "I" with the mind and body; the sense of "ownership."

Gopis: The milkmaids, childhood companions, and devotees of Krishna. They represent the world at large, whereas Krishna represents consciousness. Gopis are revered as the embodiment of the ideal state of ecstatic devotion to God.

Japa: Recitation of a mantra, or the name of the Lord.

Jivanmukta: He who has realized the truth of the oneness of the self with Brahman and the whole universe. Such people are *in* the world but not *of* the world.

Karma: The law of cause and effect. Applies to the actions—physical, mental, or verbal—of a previous life, this life, or a life hereafter, and explains the apparent injustices of the world.

Maharishi: A great sage.

Mantra: A sacred word or sound vested with the power to transform and protect the one who recites it.

Maya: The power that veils the real nature of the self so that the universe is seen as separate from the self, and the individual as separate from God.

Prana: The vital life force of the body.

Pranayama: Breathing exercises by which the prana's entry into the body is regulated.

Rishi: A seer of truth, a sage.

Samadhi: State of meditative union with the self; literally "being still."

Samskara: Past actions or thoughts that linger in the subconscious.

Siddhis: The eight powers that the yogi acquires through the practice of yoga.

Upanishads: Literally means "sitting at the feet of the master," they are the spiritual treatises of India that contain wisdom that is both universal and eternal. One hundred and twelve Upanishads were written in Sanskrit 3,000 years ago—13 principal Upanishads have been translated into English.

Vairagya: The absence of desire for the fruits of one's own action. It's the result of vigorous discrimination by which the seeker recognizes that pleasures derived from material gain are impermanent.

Vedanta: Literally means "end of the Vedas," and is one of the six schools of Indian philosophy that arose from discussions about the nature of the absolute, or the self.

Vedas: The four ancient, authoritative ancient scriptures regarded as divinely revealed.

Yajna: Ritualistic sacrifice. Any work done in the spirit of surrender to the Lord.

BIBLIOGRAPHY

Capra, F., *The Tao of Physics*. Boston: Shambhala Inc., 1991.

Chinmayananda, H. H., *Kathopanishad*. Mumbai, India: Chinmaya Mission Trust Publishers, 1989.

Chopra, D., *Everyday Immortality*. New York: Harmony Books, 1999.

———, *How to Know God*. New York: Harmony Books, 2000.

———, *Quantum Healing*. New York: Bantam Books, 1982.

Diamond, J., *Guns, Germs and Steel: The Fates of Human Societies*. New York: Norton, 1997.

Gaarder, J., *Sophie's World: A Novel about the History of Philosophy*. London: Orion Books, 1995.

Lal, M., *Shah Jahan*. Delhi: Vikas Publishing House, 1986.

Majumdar, A. K., *Rabindra Nath Tagore: The Poet of India*. Delhi: Indian Publishing Company, 1993.

Mascaro, J., *The Upanishads: Translations from the Sanskrit with an Introduction*. New York: Penguin Books, 1965.

Moussaieff, J. M., and McCarthy, S., *When Elephants Weep: Emotional Lives of Animals*. New York: Doubleday, 1995.

Pert, C., *Molecules of Emotions*. New York: Scribner, 1997.

Russel, P., *The Brain Book*. New York: Penguin Books, 1979.

Shearer, A., and Russell, P., *The Upanishads*. New York: Harper Colophon Books, 1978.

Singh, K., *Essays on Hinduism*. Delhi: Ratna Sagar, 1990.

Stein, B. A., *History of India*. Oxford: Blackwell Publishers, 1998.

Tagore, R. N., *Gitanjali: Song Offerings*. Delhi: Macmillan, 1913.

Toben, B., and Wolf, F. A., *In Conversation with Theoretical Physicists*. New York: Bantam Books, 1983.

Vidyalankar, P. S., *The Holy Vedas: A Golden Treasury*. Delhi: Clarion Books, 1983.

Wolf, F. A., *Star Wave, Mind Consciousness and Quantum Physics*. New York: Macmillan, 1984.

RECOMMENDED
READING

Brown, K., *The Essential Teachings of Hinduism: Daily Readings from the Sacred Texts*. London: Arrow Books, 1988.

Chopra, D., *Ageless Body, Timeless Mind: The Quantum Alternative to Growing Old*. New York: Harmony Books, 1993.

Chopra, K., *Your Life Is in Your Hands: The Path to Lasting Health and Happiness*. India: Penguin Books, 1997.

Edelman, M. W., *The Measure of Our Success: A Letter to My Children and Yours*. New York: HarperCollins, 1992.

Kohler, J., *The Reluctant Surgeon: Biography of John Hunter*. New York: Doubleday, 1960.

Mitchell, S. (Ed.), *The Enlightened Mind: An Anthology of Sacred Prose*. New York: Harper Perennial, 1991.

Parthasarthy, A., *The Vedanta Treatise*. Bombay: Vedanta Life Institute, 1984.

ABOUT

THE

AUTHOR

KRISHAN CHOPRA, M.D. (1919–2001), was a prominent Indian cardiologist. He was head of the department of medicine and cardiology at the prestigious Mool Chand Khairati Ram Hospital in New Delhi for more than 25 years. Prior to that, he was professor of medicine and chief of cardiology at A.F. Medical College, Pune.

He was chairman of the Heart Care Foundation of India, a national charitable trust engaged in continuing medical and public education programs, and was involved in professional development in higher education at the University of Delhi. He was also president of Vanaprastha Sansthan, a division of Chinmaya Mission, New Delhi, engaged in public welfare and education programs for the elderly.

Dr. Chopra was actively involved in the care and well-being of other people throughout his life. *The Mystery and Magic of Love* was his second book, and is a magnificent legacy of divine love.

NOTES

NOTES

NOTES

NOTES

NOTES

We hope you enjoyed this Hay House book.
If you would like to receive a free catalog featuring
additional Hay House books and products,
or if you would like information about the
Hay Foundation, please contact:

Hay House, Inc.
P.O. Box 5100
Carlsbad, CA 92018-5100

(760) 431-7695 or (800) 654-5126
(760) 431-6948 (fax) or (800) 650-5115 (fax)

Please visit the Hay House Website at:
www.hayhouse.com